CONTEMPORARY MAASAI BEADING

21 SIMPLE PROJECTS BASED ON TRADITIONAL DESIGNS

BECCA MARAIS
RedTribe

SCHIFFER PUBLISHING

4880 Lower Valley Road • Atglen, PA 19310

Other Schiffer Books on Related Subjects

Women Artisans of Morocco: Their Stories, Their Lives, Susan Schaefer Davis & Joe Coca, ISBN 978-0-9990-5171-9

How to Weave a Navajo Rug and Other Lessons from Spider Woman, Barbara Teller Ornelas & Lynda Pete, ISBN 978-1-7344217-0-5

Weaving with Strips: 18 Projects That Reflect the Craft, History, and Culture of Strip Weaving, Monika Künti, ISBN 978-0-7643-6323-8

Model Photography: Simon Clay

Library of Congress Control Number: 2022940632

Produced by BlueRed Press Ltd. 2022
Designed by Insight Design
Type set in Fira Sans

ISBN: 978-0-7643-6552-2
Printed in China

Published by Schiffer Publishing, Ltd.
4880 Lower Valley Road
Atglen, PA 19310
Phone: (610) 593-1777; Fax: (610) 593 2002
Email: Info@schifferbooks.com
Web: www.schifferbooks.com

For our complete selection of fine books on this and related subjects, please visit our website at www.schifferbooks.com. You may also write for a free catalog.

Schiffer Publishing's titles are available at special discounts for bulk purchases for sales promotions or premiums. Special editions, including personalized covers, corporate imprints, and excerpts, can be created in large quantities for special needs. For more information, contact the publisher.

We are always looking for people to write books on new and related subjects. If you have an idea for a book, please contact us at proposals@schifferbooks.com.

Contents

Introduction   4
The History of Maasai Beads   6
RedTribe's Artisans   7
The Maasai   12
The Maasai Tradition of Beading   13

Getting Started   14
Tools   16
Materials   17

Techniques   19
Creating a Loop   19
Creating a Seed Bead Circle   20
Attaching a Clasp or Toggle   21
Creating a Beaded Surround   22
Creating Beaded Linked Rings   24
Creating a Beaded Chain   26
Creating an Extension Chain   28

Projects   30
Asymmetric Zebra Earrings ●   32
Asymmetric Zebra Necklace ●●   36
Zebra Bracelet in Orange and Lime Green ●   42

Daisy Earrings—*Kiraposho* ●   48
Daisy-Chain Necklace ●●   52
Daisy-Chain Bracelet ●●   56

Savannah Rope Bracelet ●   58
Savannah Zebra Earrings ●●   62
Savannah Semicircle Necklace ●●●   68

Naivasha Teardrop Earrings ●   74
Naivasha Pearl Necklace—*Nalepo* ●●   78
Naivasha Pearl Bracelet ●●   82

Zebra Necklace in Blue, Turquoise, and Magenta ●   86
Zebra Bracelet in Blue, Turquoise, and Magenta ●●   90
Zebra Earrings in Blue, Turquoise, and Magenta ●●●   94

Flamingo Earrings ●   102
Flamingo Necklace ●●   106

White Arrowhead Earrings ●●   110
White Arrowhead Necklace ●●   112
White-and-Gold Geometric Cuff Bracelet ●●●   116
Arrowhead Ring Earrings ●●   124

Suppliers and About the Author   128

Difficulty

●   Beginner

●●   Intermediate

●●●   Advanced

Introduction

My journey with the Maasai community of Olorte in southern Kenya began in 2009, when I moved from my hectic life in London. Together with my husband, Hennie, and our three tiny children, we relocated to this remote and unhurried community in the Loita Hills. This was the beginning of our new life, living and working closely with these extraordinary and creative people.

Our home was five hours' drive through the hot and dusty African bush from the nearest shops and hospital—this made life tough at times. It was especially challenging when it rained. We'd have to drive through brown rivers and risk getting stuck in the viscous mud. On the plus side, we got to see multitudes of zebra, giraffe, and antelope on our way to do our everyday shopping!

Our children joined the Maasai kids at the local school. This was housed in a dilapidated wooden shack with a blackboard and a volunteer teacher from a nearby village. Baboons and goats would wander nonchalantly into the classrooms and often surprise the children.

My kids immersed themselves into this curious environment—adapting effortlessly into the Maasai culture.

I quickly found my place among the Maasai women, especially connecting through my background of art and design. I began beading with Koko, a fabulous Maasai grandmother who welcomed us into her family from the very beginning.

We worked together on beaded designs and began to create colorful jewelry, which we hoped would sell to a Western market. Our aim was to generate an income for Koko and a few of the other women in the surrounding villages.

We started with a handful of beads and one Maasai widow, sitting under the shade of some enormous fruit-bearing olsokonoi trees (*Warburgia ugandensis*). Colobus monkeys often hung unperturbed above us, making loud reverberating noises with their throats, and from time to time dropping fruit on our heads.

Now we have grown to a team of twenty women—even more when we have bigger orders to complete.

Together, we have designed hundreds of pieces of jewelry and we now sell them all over the world.

With the profits of this enterprise, we have been able to provide opportunities to empower the brightest girls through secondary education and vocational training. We have also run workshops to provide insight and education on the subject of female genital mutilation (FGM) and early marriage, to try to empower girls to make informed choices about their bodies and their futures.

We have called our enterprise RedTribe—a name given to us by one of the local Maasai leaders.

While I was beading with the women, Hennie was busy gathering a team of Maasai men; together they began to work with the community to get behind some of their own initiatives and built the Maasai Academy (a community primary school), a medical clinic, a farming project, and water projects.

Eleven years later, RedTribe has organically grown into a thriving community development team of Maasai—living life together, all while serving and empowering local people through income generation, healthcare, education, and mentoring.

The History of Maasai Beads

In the past, the Maasai would have used beads made from local materials: colorful seeds, shells, bone, and horn. The beads used today are high-quality glass seed beads from the Czech Republic.

Even though the beads are sourced from Europe, the Maasai have made them their own. They have put their own identity into the designs and uses of the beadwork they create.

The Significance of Color

Maasai beadwork is beautifully colorful, but the colors used are not just for decoration. Each one holds a significant meaning—often associated with the love of the cattle that provide so much for the Maasai.

Red is the color of blood—it is a symbol of courage and strength, but also the blood of the cow that is slaughtered during important ceremonies.

Orange and **yellow** are the colors of fire—and represent warmth and hospitality. It is on the fire that the food and *chai* (tea) are cooked to share.

Green is the color of grass—symbolizing health and the grazing land for the cattle that sustain the Maasai.

Blue is the color of the sky and symbolizes energy. Rain comes from the sky and provides water for the Maasai and their cattle.

White is the color of their cows' milk and signifies purity. The Maasai consider their cows to be pure and holy animals.

Black symbolizes unity and solidarity. The struggles they undergo bring them together as a people.

RedTribe's Artisans

The Maasai artisans gather together every weekday afternoon to create beaded designs for RedTribe.

Even though they have had their own workshop specially built, you will often find them sitting outside under the cooling shade of an acacia tree as they do their beading.

There is a constant buzz of chatter, and always laughter and singing. Both young and old are dressed in traditional colorful robes and layers of beadwork with tiny silver disks hanging from them, so they sparkle as they reflect the sunlight. They are altogether a beautiful group of women.

Their difficult circumstances do not define them. Each one of them seems to have an inspiring air of poise and serenity. They wear resilience and determination with great dignity. Let me introduce them to you.

Koko is our oldest artisan—claiming she has reached the ripe old age of two hundred!

She remembers the times when the tribe was still fully nomadic, living in very temporary huts. She wandered the plains and hills with her cattle and community in search of good pasture. She is a huge character known by everyone in the region and beyond. When there is a drought in an area, Koko is taken there in the belief that rain will come.

Koko has been here right from the beginning, helping us to pioneer the enterprise. She would sometimes drink one too many of the local honey beer brewed from honey and aloe vera (as is customary for the older people), and would go on to create the craziest but most whimsical jewelry, which would then become one of our bestsellers! Among other designs, Koko helped create the Savannah Semicircle Necklace. She is our grandmother, and she brings love and loads of laughter to the team!

Kiraposho works hard to provide for her family without help from her husband, because he has a severe learning disability. Life is tough for Kiraposho, but she remains strong and determined and is a valuable asset to RedTribe. She is responsible for helping Nalotwesha to make the beautiful beaded chains used on the necklaces.

Naisula is a valuable member of the team, working quietly alongside the other artisans. She is one of two wives and lives nearby her cowife. She has many children whom she provides for. She is especially keen to make sure they have an education, and uses much of her income to pay their fees. Naisula helps make our Daisy-Chain necklaces.

Melau is a young and talented woman. She is one of two wives with five children and has undergone FGM and early marriage. Despite these difficult circumstances, Melau is full of fun and has a mischievous streak, which makes everyone laugh out loud! She's also a talented beader and will often help create new designs. She is responsible for making the more complicated beaded circle earrings and necklaces.

Noolari was subjected to FGM and an early arranged marriage to a man she did not choose. She is still a young woman but has several great-grandchildren. She lives in the most traditional Maasai hut on the top of the highest hill—making it a difficult place to carry water and wood to.

Noolari wears her resilience with poise and dignity. She is a kind and gentle woman and a wonderful mother. Her creativity and artisan skills are outstanding. Noolari is responsible for making RedTribe's rope bracelets and the Naivasha Pearl collection.

Noolepeta is a strong and hugely capable woman. She works with absolute precision with a keen eye for detail, making sure her work is of the highest quality. She has five children and is determined to send each one to school to give them a good future. Noolepeta has created RedTribe's beaded cuff bangle and White Arrowhead earrings, as well as the Savannah Semicircle Necklace.

Noolkitoip is a strong and dignified woman who always wears the most beautiful beadwork. She is one of three wives; her husband spends months away at a time because his two other wives live in different areas. She has six children and has to provide for them without help from her husband.

Noolkitoip walks miles across the Loita Hills to come to work with RedTribe. Despite her tough situation, she has a wonderful sense of humor and is warm and generous. Noolkitoip is responsible for making RedTribe's triangle earrings—such as the green zebra triangles in the Savannah Zebra Collection.

Noolturot is one of five wives and has seven children, and life is a struggle for her. Her work at RedTribe has been important since she has little or no financial help from her husband. He is a traditional man who values his cows more than his wives and children. Noolturot is always cheerful and values her time beading and chatting with the other artisans. She makes decorations and has helped create the White Arrowhead collection.

Nalotwesha is wise and gentle. She lost her twelve-year-old son a few years ago, leaving her brokenhearted, but her inspiring faith and hope in Enkai (the supreme creator in Maasai mythology) has given her a strength and serenity. She is a notable woman and an example to so many around her. Nalotwesha is responsible for making beaded chains, attaching clasps, and creating extensions for RedTribe's designs.

Sikar is a young woman with seven children. She has to work extremely hard to provide for her family. She does extra work collecting and carrying excruciatingly heavy bundles of firewood for other women so that she can make sure she can cover the cost of her children's school fees. She is a new member of RedTribe's team of artisans and has a natural talent for beading. Sikar has helped create the Flamingo collection.

Nalepo is our closest artisan. Living in the nearby village, she has to walk only a short distance through the river to work. Her husband was attacked by a lion many years ago, and although he survived he has been left disabled, so her work is important for her family. She has ten children and the kindest heart. Nalepo helps finish RedTribe's designs and also makes daisy earrings and bracelets.

Nomtinanna is our beadwork manager and also helps create the threaded beaded necklaces and bracelets for RedTribe. She has overcome many obstacles to get where she is now; like so many others she has not been able to make choices of her own. Even with limited education, and having undergone FGM as well as an unwanted, arranged marriage, she has—with great faith, determination, and hard work—become a strong and empowered woman and role model, who brilliantly manages our team of artisans. She trained in educating women about the harmful practice of FGM and has used her knowledge to help eradicate this practice as far as is possible. She is extremely intelligent and organized, and RedTribe is so privileged to have Nomtinanna on the team.

Noolmishuki is our youngest artisan. She has four little children and her husband has a learning disability, so working with RedTribe brings really important income to her family. She has invested her earnings in a donkey which helps her carry water more easily—giving her extra time and energy to manage her work and family. Since becoming part of the RedTribe team, she has grown in faith, joy, and confidence. She joined the team without many beading skills, but she has learned so much from the artisans and is now able to produce beautiful work. She makes many of the beaded surround bracelets produced by RedTribe.

The Maasai

The Maasai are probably one of the most notable tribes in the whole of Africa. Cloaked in red and draped with beads, they look almost royal in their attire. This dignified pastoral people, rich in culture and tradition, have roamed their cattle over the plains of Kenya and Tanzania for hundreds of years.

They are particularly known for their fierce and elaborately decorated young warriors.

"A Maasai warrior is a fine sight. Those young men have, to the utmost extent, that particular form of intelligence which we call chic; daring and wildly fantastical as they seem, they are still unswervingly true to their own nature, and to an immanent ideal. Their style is not an assumed manner, or an imitation of a foreign perfection; it has grown from the inside and is an expression of the race and its history, and their weapons and finery are as much a part of their being as are a stag's antlers." —Karen Blixen

The Maasai have built up a collection of beaded jewelry over the years. They often wear layer upon layer of necklaces, which adds to their already striking apperance. The layered necklaces, with tiny metal disks hung from each piece, clink together as they move and make a sound that becomes an unmistakable characteristic of the women. When you create your pieces of jewelry, you could also layer them by making several of the same design and altering the lengths, or by layering different designs, adding interest and texture to an outfit.

For me, though, it is the women, whom I have grown to love and respect so much over the years of living and working there. Their joyful resilience, warmth, and generosity are always overwhelming and something to aspire to. What strikes me too is that whatever they are doing, whether it be carrying water or chopping wood—regardless of age—they always make sure they look as beautiful as possible.

Layers of colors and patterned cloth, with tiers of carefully crafted beadwork, are their fabulous everyday attire.

The Maasai Tradition of Beading

Maasai women have been beading for centuries.

The Maasai do not wear beaded jewelry purely to enhance their beauty, but also as a way to display important aspects of their cultural identity. Jewelry is worn to indicate age and social status, as well as to mark an important event or rite of passage. For example, a bride traditionally wears a highly decorative, beaded headdress and extravagantly layered necklaces for her ceremony.

The color and style of their beadwork might also indicate which area they are from; for example, the Maasai women of the Loita Hills often use white beads to make their jewelry. Fashion can also dictate what beadwork the women might wear—this of course changes according to what the latest trends are at the time!

Traditionally, it was considered the role of the women to make the beaded jewelry, so it was the most natural thing in the world for the women to want to become the artisans of RedTribe.

As the Maasai culture is gradually being pressured to change by an ever-encroaching developing world, many of their traditions are getting lost. RedTribe believes in conserving the rich cultural heritage and beading skills of the Maasai, which have been their mark of beauty and identity for centuries.

Getting Started

Getting Started
Tools

1. **Beading awl** This is the favorite tool of many Maasai artisans. They usually make their own beading awl (*oltidu* in *Maa*—the Maasai language) by taking a spoke from an old umbrella and breaking it to the length they require. They then sharpen the ends into finely tapered points with a file. Next, they push one end into a thin branch, which they use as a handle. It's used for most of their beading techniques since it is the most accessible tool they have. If they lose it, they can easily make another.

   It's used to make the tiny loops in a chain link. However, you can also use the tapered end of roundnose pliers to do the job if you want to. You can also use it to pierce through the recycled plastic in your beaded cuff or circle earrings.

2. **Bent chain-nose pliers** These can be used as an alternative to the roundnose pliers to make loops. They can also be useful when using nylon-coated beading wire—to help you feed the wire back through a beading crimp. It's fiddly carrying out this task, and these will give you more control.

3. **Craft knife** For carefully cutting the pieces of recycled plastic used to create the beaded cuff and beaded circle earrings.

4. **End cutters** Maasai artisans tend to break the wire instead of using wire cutters, since this helps avoid the sharp ends created when you use cutters. However, when the wire is thicker, you might need to use them. Always remember to file the wire point to soften it and avoid any scratchy ends.

5. **File** This is used to soften the sharp ends of wire that you get when you use wire cutters. It will help avoid any irritating scratchy ends, which can be uncomfortable and even cut skin when you are wearing your piece of jewelry.

6. **Roundnose pliers** These pliers are characterized by their rounded, tapering jaws. They are used to make loops with the beading wire. Because the ends are tapered, you can vary the size of your loops. For the tiny loops used to create the chain link, you can use the very end of your roundnose pliers. For the larger loops (for example, the loops you might make to feed your chain through), you can use the wider end of the pliers, nearer the handles.

7. **Serrated flat-nose pliers** These flat-nosed pliers have tapered jaws that are serrated on their flat inner surfaces. They can be used to grip your wire and pull it tight, if it's difficult using your fingers. The artisans tend to use their fingers, since they are well practiced and have therefore developed enormous strength.

8. **Smooth flat-nose pliers** Used to straighten or make bends in the wire.

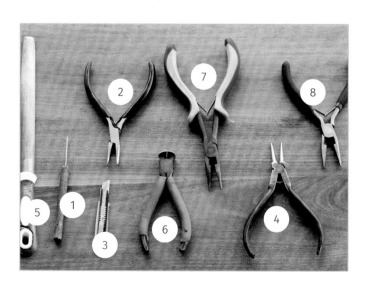

Materials

1. **Bead end caps** Used to finish RedTribe's beaded rope bracelet. They secure and cover the end of the beaded rope: the central wire is fed through the eye of the cap and secured with a loop, which is then used to attach findings.

2. **Brass crimp beads** Soft metal beads used to secure the loops made with the nylon beaded wire. They can also act as a bead stopper.

3. **Gold-plated earring hooks** These are hypoallergenic.

4. **Handmade 2 mm Ethiopian brass beads** Used in all of RedTribe's designs, they are shiny when polished. They are elegant at the same time as being rustic.

5. **Brass hard wire, 22 gauge** This is much less flexible and is used for straight or angled lengths on your piece of jewelry.

6. **Brass hard wire, 24 gauge** This hard wire is used to make larger rings. It is less bendable, so keeps its shape more easily.

7. **Lobster clasps** A finding used as an attachment for both necklaces and the finer bracelets.

8. **Brass soft wire, 24 gauge** Commonly used to make chain links. The wire needs to be soft and flexible so as to be able to make the small loops required for chain, using the beading awl or roundnose pliers.

9. **Toggle clasp** This finding consists of a metal bar that goes through a loop. It is used as a bracelet attachment.

10. **Brass very soft wire, 26 gauge** Fine, super-flexible wire used to wind through beaded wire to keep the bead patterns in place.

11. **Black and white, 11/0 (about 1.8 mm) glass seed beads** These are used in several designs to create an authentic Maasai tribal feel.

12. **Freshwater pearls, 6–7 mm and 8–9 mm** Used in RedTribe's Naivasha collection.

13. **Gold, 6 mm stardust beads** These are small brass beads with a textured surface creating a sparkly effect. They are used in several of RedTribe's designs.

14. **Lime green, 11/0 (about 1.8 mm) glass seed beads** Used in RedTribe's Savannah collection.

15. **Rope, approximately 6 mm diameter** Used to make RedTribe's Savannah Rope Bracelet. A hard wire is fed through the center of the rope, and a beaded wire is then wound evenly around the rope in coils. Finally, it is finished with beaded end caps and attachments.

16. **Turquoise, 11/0 (about 1.8 mm) glass seed beads** Tiny turquoise seed beads are used in several designs.

17. **White, 7–8/0 (about 2.9 mm) glass seed beads** Used to surround the yellow central bead in our Daisy Earrings.

18. **White and black plastic water bottles** The Maasai recycle their old water containers to make the dividers for holding the beaded wires in place on some of the designs. They are cut into strips by using a craft knife and pierced to create tiny holes for the beaded wire to run through.

19. **Yellow, 6/0 (about 3 mm) glass seed beads** These are the central beads used to make RedTribe's Daisy collection.

20. **Yellow, orange, pink, 6 mm glass beads** The yellow beads are used to make RedTribe's Daisy Earrings. The orange and pink beads are used in our Asymmetric collection.

Techniques
Creating a Loop

This is probably the most important technique you need to learn. It underpins the majority of designs you will make!

I have used our Naivasha Pearl Necklace (page 78) as an example of the process.

The same principle can be used to make the loops needed for attaching earring hooks, as well as the links used to create our beaded chains, bracelets, and necklaces.

Tools
Roundnose pliers

Materials
24-gauge wire

1. Hold the roundnose pliers using either your left or right hand—depending on which is more comfortable. Take the length of wire you are using to create a loop, then pinch it tightly with the roundnose pliers.

2. Bend the wire into a loop shape by wrapping the wire tightly all the way around one of the pins of your roundnose pliers.

3. Once you have made a loop, stretch the wire across (3a). Wind it tightly around itself to secure it (3b). Break off any excess wire by wiggling it back and forth until it breaks easily. (3c)

4. Once you have created your loop, feed the chain through so it can hang freely.

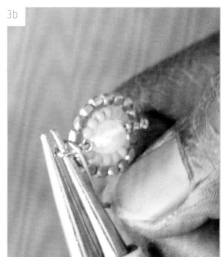

Creating a Seed Bead Circle

Materials

Seed beads
24-gauge hard wire
24-gauge soft wire

1. Thread one seed bead onto a length of 24-gauge hard wire. Note that this is your central wire.

2. Take a second piece of wire—this time using 24-gauge soft wire—and attach it to your central wire by winding it tightly around. Break off any excess wire from one end, leaving a length of wire to thread your seed beads onto. Thread two or three seed beads and carefully bend your beaded wire halfway around your central seed bead.

3. Now attach the beaded wire to the central wire, by once again winding the wire tightly around the central hard wire.

4. Thread a few more seed beads onto the soft wire and carefully bend the beaded wire around the other side of the central seed bead. Attach it to the central wire in the same way you did before.

5. Continue to thread seed beads onto the soft wire.

6. Bend the beaded wire around the previous row of beads and attach them to the central wire in the same way you have been doing. Continue with the same process until you have two rows of seed beads surrounding your central bead. Attach the wire and break off any excess.

Attaching a Clasp or Toggle

Tools
Beading awl
Roundnose pliers

Materials
Handmade 2 mm Ethiopian brass beads
Lobster clasp
Toggle clasp
24-gauge wire

1. On one end of your chain or bracelet, attach a length of wire. Using roundnose pliers, gently pinch the wire and wrap it around one end of the pliers to make a tiny loop. Cross over the wire and secure the loop by winding the wire once around itself. Break off any excess leaving a length of wire. Onto your wire, thread a 2 mm brass bead and your clasp. (see page 26,27)

2. Create a loop by bending the wire around. (2, insert)

3. Cross the wire over itself—just above the bead.

4. Wind the wire tightly around itself. (You can use a beading awl or roundnose pliers.) Break off any excess wire.

5. You can attach your clasp to either a necklace chain (5) or a beaded bracelet, using exactly the same method (insert).

6. You can use a toggle clasp as an alternative to a lobster clasp for your bracelet (although note that you can't add an extension chain to this). Use exactly the same method to attach it.

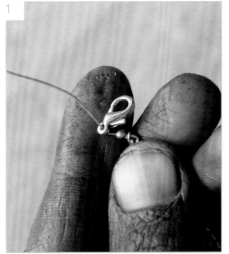

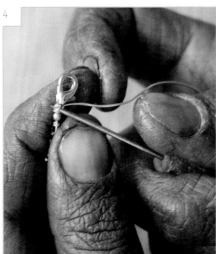

Creating a Beaded Surround

Materials
Central bead
Seed beads
24-gauge wire

1. Thread your central bead onto a length of 24-gauge hard wire. (1a)

   Take a length of 22- or 24-gauge soft wire and wind it tightly around the central wire to attach it securely. (1b)

2. Break off any excess soft wire, leaving about a 7.8 in. (20 cm) length to work with.

3. Now thread seed beads onto the soft wire.

4. Next, carefully bend the beaded wire half around the central bead.

5. Now wind the soft wire all the way around your central wire. (5a, 5b, 5c)

6. Thread more seed beads onto the soft wire and carefully bend it around the other side of the central bead.

7. Once you have surrounded your central bead, wind the beaded wire tightly around the central wire, then break off any excess wire.

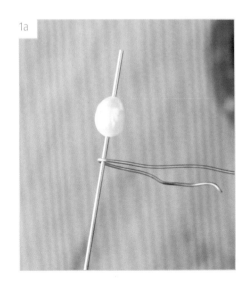

1a

Creating Beaded Linked Rings

Tools
Roundnose pliers

Materials
Handmade 2 mm Ethiopian brass beads
24-gauge wire

1. Thread a row of 2mm brass beads onto a length of 24-gauge hard brass wire.

2. Carefully bend the beaded wire into a 1–1.2 in. (2.5–3 cm) diameter circle. Cross over the wire.

3. Bend one end of the beaded wire over the other and wind it once around to secure it together. (3a)

   Wiggle the end of the wire you have used to wind around the other end, and break it off so you have a circle with a length of wire left. (3b)

   Repeat the process and create another beaded ring about half the size.

4. Next, pull the wire back out of the tiny attachment loop you have just created (by winding the wire around itself) and link it to your second beaded ring. Now feed the remaining length of wire back through the tiny attachment loop.

5. Create a loop on both rings, using the length of wire left. (5a, 5b, 5c)

6. These linked rings can be adapted and used in several designs.

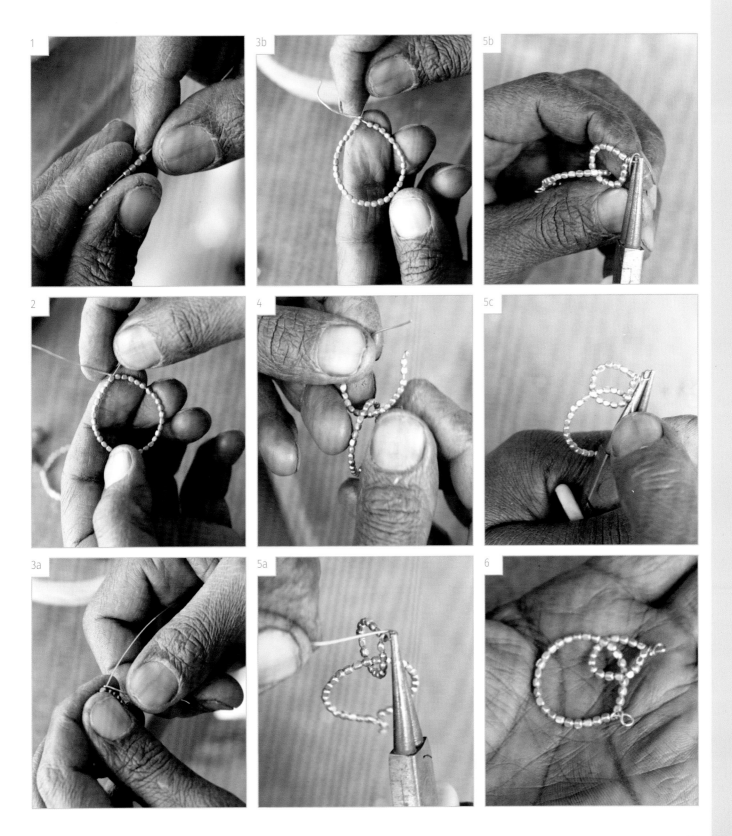

Creating a Beaded Chain

Tools
Roundnose pliers

Materials
Handmade 2 mm Ethiopian brass beads
24-gauge soft brass wire

1. Take about a 5.9 in. (15 cm) length of 24-gauge soft brass wire. Using roundnose pliers, gently pinch the wire and wrap it around one end of the pliers to make a tiny loop.

2. Cross over the wire and secure the loop by winding the wire once around itself. Break off any excess wire, leaving a length of wire to thread your bead onto, and enough to make the next loop. (2a, 2b, 2c, 2d)

3. Next, thread a 2 mm brass bead onto the wire and make another loop, using the same technique as you did before.

4. To create a chain link, thread another 5.9 in. or so length of wire through one of the loops you've created, and begin the process of creating a loop again—using the same technique as you did in step 2. (4a, 4b)

5. Continue this process until you have created a beautiful beaded chain.

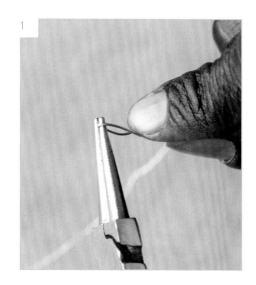

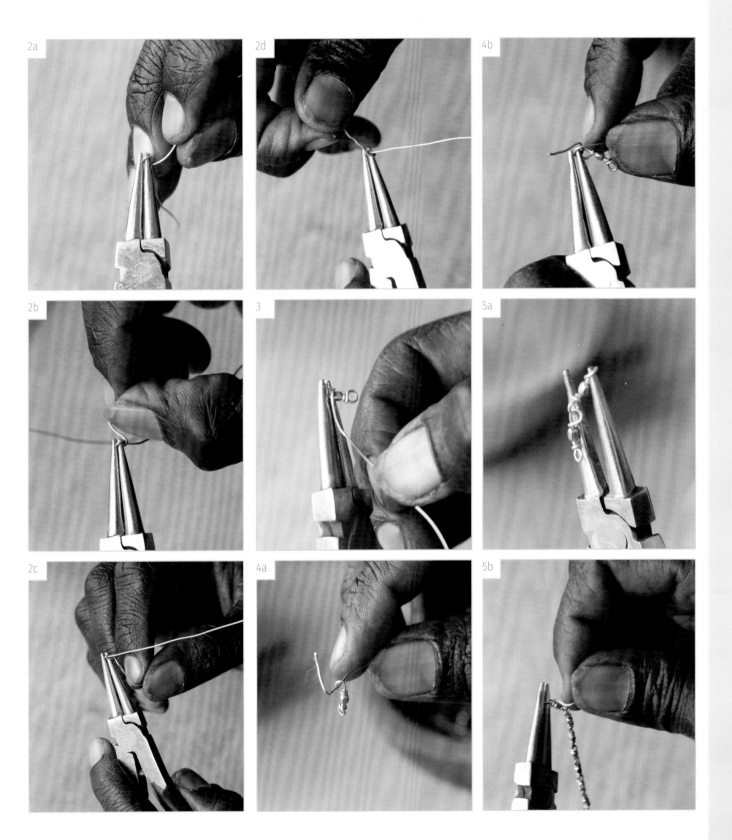

Creating an Extension Chain

Once you have completed your chain (or bracelet), you might want to create an extension chain to make your piece of jewelry more versatile. An extension chain will enable you to wear the same piece of jewelry with several different necklines. It will also mean it can be worn comfortably by people of different sizes.

Tools
Beading awl
Roundnose pliers

Materials
Seed beads
24-gauge wire

1. At the end of your chain, begin by attaching a length of 24-gauge soft brass wire in the same way as you did to make the chain. Add a bead—the type of bead will depend on the necklace or bracelet—for example, you will need to use a white seed bead on your daisy-chain necklace. In this example, our artisan has used a 2 mm brass bead. (1a)

   Now, using your roundnose pliers, pinch the wire and create a loop a little larger than your chain link (refer to page 19). This will make it much easier to close your clasp onto. Break off any excess wire.

2. Again, attach a length of wire to your loop. In this image, our artisan is using a beading awl to make a tiny loop. (2a)

   Now add a bead to the wire. (2b)

3. Immediately after your bead, create another loop, again a little larger than your chain link. Break off any excess wire.

4. Continue this process until you are happy with the length of the extension chain. Our artisans will often create three or four larger loops and then finish off by adding a tag—but this is not essential. (4a, 4b, 4c)

5. Here's an example of a dais- chain extension using white seed beads.

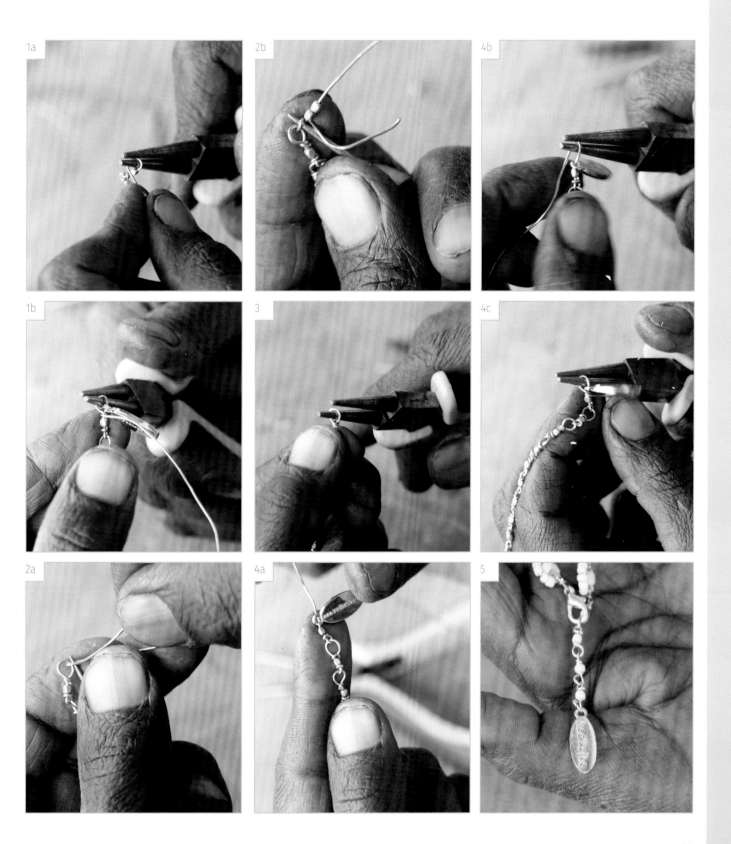

Asymmetric Zebra Earrings ●

Created by Melau

TOOLS & MATERIALS

Roundnose pliers
Beading awl

Black and white glass seed beads, 11/0
   (1.8 mm)
Handmade 2 mm Ethiopian brass beads
Matt pink glass bead, 6–8 mm
Orange glass bead, 6 mm
24-gauge hard wire
24-gauge soft wire

1. Take a length of hard brass 24-gauge wire and scoop up a row of small brass beads (3 mm) .

2. Carefully bend the beaded wire into a 0.8–1.2 in. (2.5–3 cm) diameter circle.

3. Take one end of the beaded wire and wind it twice around the other end of the wire to secure them together. Wiggle the end of the wire you have used to wind around the other end, and break it off so you have a circle with a length of wire left.

4. Make a loop, using the length of wire on the circle (see page 19).

5. The next step is to create a smaller ring of black and white seed beads to hang from the gold ring you have just created.

   First scoop your black and white beads onto some 24-gauge hard wire. Black, then white, then black, and so on.

6. Carefully bend the black-and-white-beaded wire into a 0.4–0.6 in. (1–1.5 cm) diameter circle.

7. Take one end of the wire and wind it around the other end of the wire twice, to tie it together and create a ring. Wiggle the end of the wire you have used to wind around the other end, then break it off, so you have a circle with a length of wire.

8. Next, pull the wire back out of the tiny attachment loop you have created, and link it to your gold ring as shown.

9. Reattach your black and white circle by pushing the wire back through the tiny loop. You should now have two circles linked together (as shown in the photograph).

10. Create another loop on the smaller black and white loop, using the same method.

11. Now feed a hairpin through the eye of a 6 mm pink glass bead and then through the loop on the gold ring.

12. Attach the pink bead by winding the head pin around itself and create a tiny loop, using your roundnose pliers or an *oltedo*. Break off the excess wire (see page 19).

    Finally, attach your earring hook, twist the loop open with a pair of pliers, and hook your drop earring design onto the wire, before closing the loop again. You will have made the first of your pair of asymmetric earrings.

13. Repeat the process to create the other earring. But this time, use black and white seed beads for the larger of the two rings, and brass beads for the smaller ring. Attach an orange bead to the larger ring and an earring hook to the smaller ring, and you will have created a beautiful pair of earrings.

These are the skills you need to make some colorful and fun asymmetric earrings!

All the projects are presented in sets, and the color bands alongside the step-by-step instructions indicate each collection.

These—and the next two projects—are part of our Zebra collection.

Asymmetric Zebra Necklace ●●

Created by Melau

TOOLS & MATERIALS

Beading awl
Roundnose pliers

Black and white glass seed beads,
    11/0 (1.8 mm)
Gold stardust beads, 3 x 6 mm
Handmade 2 mm Ethiopian brass beads
Matt pink glass bead, 6 mm or 8 mm
Orange glass bead, 6 mm
24-gauge hard wire
24-gauge soft wire

1. Begin with a length of 24-gauge hard wire, and thread onto it a row of alternating black and white 2 mm seed beads.

2. Create a ring of about 0.8–1.2 in. (2–3 cm) diameter and attach it together by winding the wire tightly around itself.

3. Leave enough length of wire to create a loop.

4. Create a loop, using the method on page 19. With either a beading awl or some roundnose pliers, break off any excess wire.

5. Next, thread a row of brass beads onto a length of 24-gauge wire and bend it into a smaller ring of approximately 0.6 in. (1.5 cm) diameter.

6. Attach it together, leaving a length of wire long enough to create another loop later.

7. Link the two rings together (see pages 24-25).

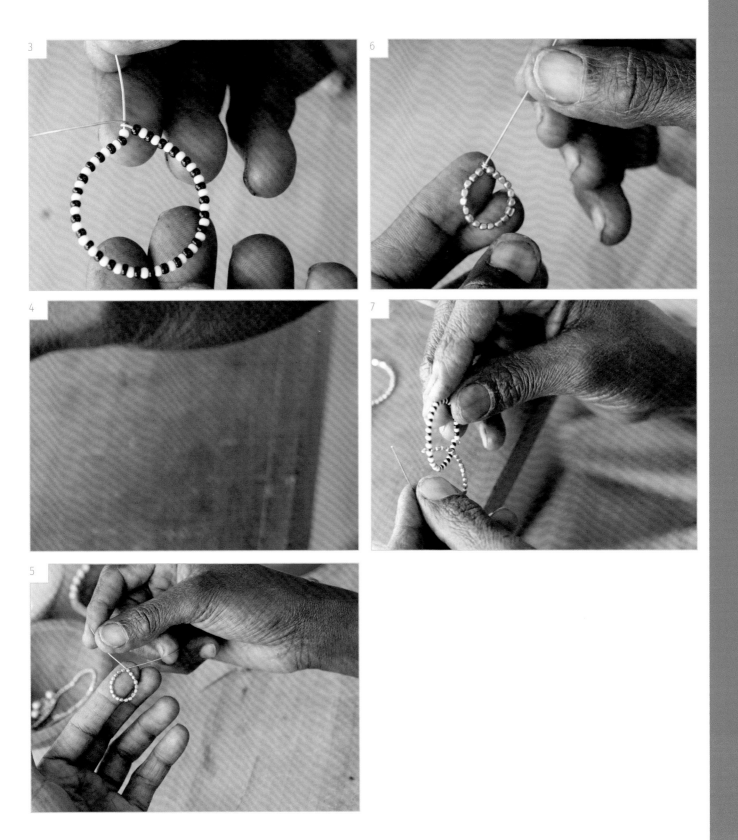

8. Now that the rings are linked together, create a loop on the brass ring and break off any excess wire. (8a, 8b)

9. Next, attach a 6 mm gold stardust bead to the loop on the black and white ring (see pages 26-27). Create another loop ready for the next bead.

10. Link another 6 mm gold stardust bead to the first bead.

11. Now link a third 6 mm gold stardust bead to the previous one.

12. Add a final loop to hold your 6 mm gold stardust bead in place.

Now you are ready to attach your chain.

13. Next, link a length of hard wire to the smaller brass-beaded ring.

14. Leave a length of wire ready to thread through your next bead.

15. Thread an orange 6 mm glass bead though the wire attached to the brass ring.

8a

8b

9

16. Create a loop on the wire threaded through the orange bead ready to attach your next bead.

17. Attach a length of wire to the loop holding the orange bead by creating another loop. Then thread a pink 6 mm or 8 mm glass bead onto it.

18. Make another loop to hold the pink bead in place.

19. Attach your chain to the wire loop holding the pink bead in place.

20. In the same way, attach your chain to the wire loop holding the 6 mm gold bead in place. Finally, attach your lobster clasp and extension chain.

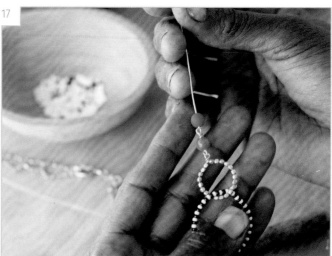

Zebra Bracelet in Orange and Lime Green ●

Created by Nontinanna

TOOLS & MATERIALS

Beading awl
Flat-nose pliers
Roundnose pliers
Wire cutters

Black and white seed beads, 11/0 (1.8 mm)
Brass crimping beads
Brass head pin or 24-gauge hard wire
Handmade 2 mm Ethiopian brass beads
Lime or orange beads, 11/0 (1.8 mm)
Nylon-coated beading wire
Matte pink glass bead, 6 mm
24-gauge soft wire

1. Cut a length of nylon beading wire about 9.8 in. (25 cm) long and thread a beading crimp onto it.

2. Feed one end of the wire back through the tiny crimp bead to create a loop.

3. Use your flat-nose pliers to pinch the bead tightly to secure it. (3a, 3b)

4. Take the open end of your beading wire and thread about 2.7–3 in. (7–8 cm) of 2mm brass beads onto it.

5. Continue to thread 1.5–1.7 in. (4–4.5 cm) of black and white seed beads onto your beading wire. Following this, thread three 2 mm brass beads.

6. Next, thread about 1.5–1.7 in. (4–4.5 cm) of either your orange seed beads or your lime seed beads, depending on the color you prefer.

7. Your pattern is now complete.

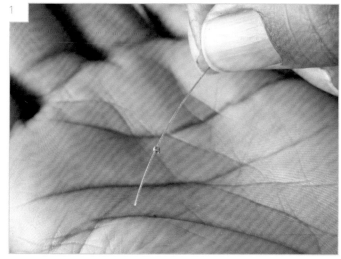

8. Now secure your beads by creating another loop on the open end of your beading wire. Use the same technique as you did in steps 2 and 3 on page 42. (8a)

This process is a bit fiddly, so be patient with yourself! (8b)

Make sure you tuck the end of the wire into the beads, to avoid any scratchy ends. (8c)

9. Repeat the whole process again—following the same pattern to create a second row of beads. Again, make loops on both ends of the wire. Now thread a piece of soft brass wire through the loops on the lime or orange-beaded ends of both beaded wires.

10. Now attach the wire by creating a chain link (see pages 28-29). Thread a brass bead onto it, ready for your extension chain. Then make an extension chain (see pages 28-29).

11. Take a head pin or a piece of 24-gauge wire—with the end bent and pinched to create a bead stop. (11a, 11b, 11c)

12. Attach the 6 mm pink glass bead to the end of your extension chain (with a tag if you want), using a loop (see page 19).

8a

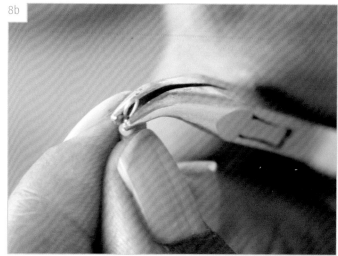

8b

8c

13. Now you have completed one end of your bracelet. Here we have used one of our special RedTribe brass tags.

14. Take the other ends of the bracelet and thread a piece of soft 24-gauge wire through the loops.

15. Attach the wire, add a brass bead, and create one chain link (see pages 26-27). (16a, 16b)

16. Finally, complete your design by attaching a lobster clasp (see page 21). (17a, 17b)

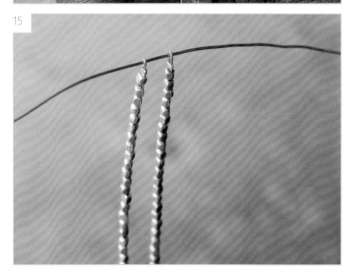

16a

16b

17a

17b

Daisy Earrings ●

Created by Nalepo

TOOLS & MATERIALS

Beading awl
Roundnose pliers
Wire cutters

Brass head pins x 2 or 24-gauge hard wire.
 (about 5.9 in. / 15 cm long)
Yellow glass beads, 2 x 6 mm
White glass seed beads, 7-8/0 (2.9 mm)
24-gauge soft wire (about 11.8 in. / 3 0cm long)

1. Thread a 6 mm yellow glass bead onto a brass head pin or hard 24-gauge wire.

   Next, take a length of soft 24-gauge wire and attach it to the head pin by winding it tightly around the pin.

2. Thread a row of 2 mm white glass seed beads onto the soft wire attached to the pin.

3. Carefully bend the beaded wire halfway around the central yellow bead.

4. Attach the beaded wire to the pin by winding the soft wire around it once or twice.

5. Thread some more white 2 mm seed beads onto the same soft wire.

6. Again, bend the beaded wire around the other side of the yellow central bead until it is completely surrounded by white beads. The beads will begin to look like the petals around the center of a daisy.

7. Next, holding the beaded wire in place . . . (7a)

   . . . wind it tightly around the pin to attach it. (7b)

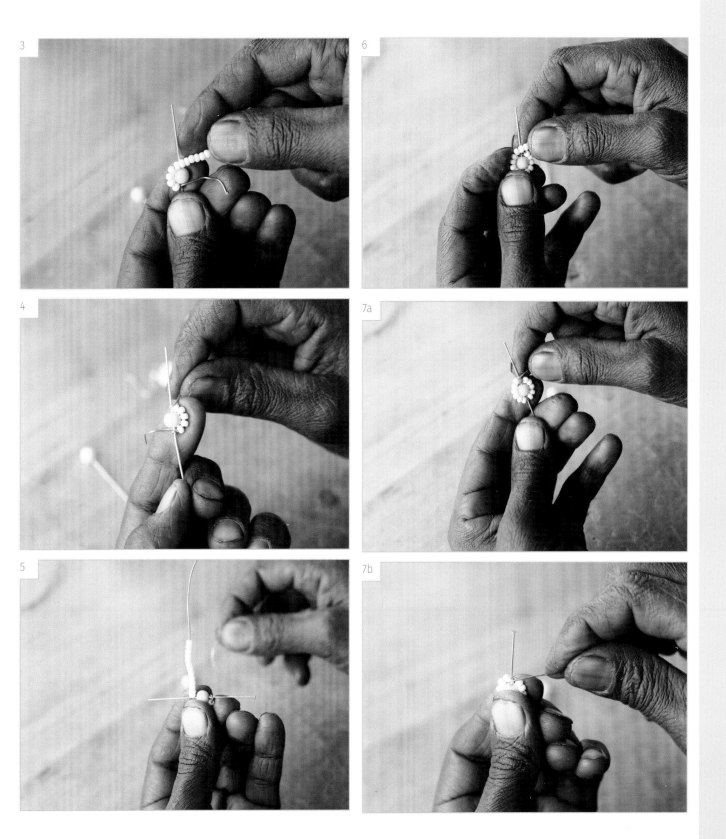

8. Remove the excess wire by gently wiggling it back and forth . . . (8a)

   . . . until it breaks easily. (8b)

9. Now, create a loop, using roundnose pliers or beading awl (see pages 19–20). (9a, 9b)

10. Bend the head pin around the end of the pliers and wind it tightly around itself. Break off any excess wire by cutting (since this is hard wire, it is much more difficult to break) or wiggling it if you have strong fingers!

11. Repeat the process to create a pair of daisy earrings. Finally, attach the earring hooks. (See step 12, page 34)

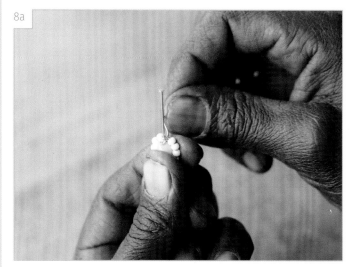

8a

8b

9a

9b

10

11

Daisy-Chain Necklace ●●

Created by Naisula

TOOLS & MATERIALS

Beading awl
Roundnose pliers

Lobster clasp
White 11/0 (1.8 mm) seed beads
Yellow 6/0 (4 mm) seed beads
24-gauge hard wire
24-gauge soft wire

1. Thread several 3 mm yellow glass seed beads onto a 11.8 in. (30 cm) length or so of hard brass wire—this is your central wire. However, it doesn't matter too much how much wire you use at this stage, since you are making a chain of daisies, meaning you can add lengths of wire as, and when, you need.

   Take another length of brass wire, but this time soft 24 gauge. Thread several white 1.5 mm seed beads onto it.

2. Wind your white-beaded wire tightly around the central wire to attach it.

   Now bend the beaded wire halfway around your central yellow bead.

3. Attach the white-beaded wire to the central wire by winding it tightly around it in the same way as you did in step 2.

4. Thread a few more white beads onto the soft wire and complete your beaded surround.

5. In the same way as before, attach this beaded wire to the central wire to secure it.

6. Break off any excess wire.

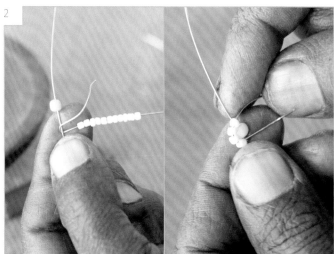

7. Using the same method, continue to create beaded daisies along your central wire.

For the short daisy chain, you will need to make approximately twenty-four daisies.

8. At the end of the row of daisies, make a loop with the central wire to start your chain. (8a, 8b, 8c, 8d)

In these photographs, RedTribe artisan Noolari has used a traditional Maasai beading awl, but you can also use some roundnose pliers if you find it easier (personally, I do!)—see pages 26-27 for the method.

9. Pull your daisy right up to the loop you have made, and create a loop on the other side of it. It is easier to do this if you pull all the other daisies away from the part of the wire you are working on.

Once you have created a loop on both sides of the daisy, you can break off the wire.

10. Now feed your central wire (with all your daisies pulled to one end) through the loop you have made, and link it together by creating another loop. Pull the next daisy up to the loop and begin the process again. Continue until you have completed your daisy chain. (10a, 10b)

You can create any length of chain. For a short necklace, you can add an extension chain and lobster clasp, while for a long chain you can just continue creating daisies. When you are happy with the length, join both ends of your necklace together.

11. Attach a lobster clasp at one end of the daisy chain. (11a, 11b)

12. At the other end, create an extension chain, using white beads at regular intervals between your loops. (12a, 12b)

To create a layered look, you can wind the necklace around your neck several times. Or make another!

8a

8b

8c

8d

9

10a

10b

12b

11a

11b

12a

Daisy-Chain Bracelet ●●

Created by Nalepo

TOOLS & MATERIALS

Beading awl or roundnose pliers

Toggle clasp
White seed beads, 11/0 (1.8 mm)
Yellow glass seed beads, 6/0 (4 mm)
24-gauge soft wire

1. To create this Daisy Chain Bracelet, you use exactly the same method as you did to create your Daisy Chain Necklace. The only difference is the length of the daisy chain and the clasp you use.

   To make a medium-size bracelet, we suggest you make a length of daisy links between 7.4 and 8.3 in. (19–21 cm). This will be about twelve daisy links.

2. Taking a length of wire (a few inches will do) at the end of the daisy chain, attach the bar of your toggle clasp (see page 21). (1a, 1b, 1c, 1d)

3. In the same way, attach the ring on the other end of the daisy chain. (2a, 2b)

4. You can easily pull the bar through the ring component to secure your bracelet in place.

5. It is easier to hook and unhook a toggle clasp with one hand than a lobster clasp. However, a lobster clasp can also work as a bracelet attachment—especially on a finer bracelet.

1a

1b

1c

3

2a

2b

Savannah Rope Bracelet ●

Createc by Noolari

TOOLS & MATERIALS

Roundnose pliers
Wire cutters

Black and white seed beads, 11/0 (1.8 mm)
Handmade 2 mm Ethiopian brass beads
Lime-green seed beads, 11/0 (1.8 mm)
Rope or cord, 6 mm diameter
24-gauge hard wire
26-gauge wire

1. Take a length of 24-gauge hard wire and feed it carefully through the center of about a 7.8 in. (20 cm) long, 6 mm diameter rope or strong cord.

2. Push the wire all the way through until you reach the other end of the rope, then pull it evenly all the way through to the other side.

3. Take a long length (approximately 32 in. / 80 cm) of very soft, 26-gauge wire, and thread up a row of lime-green 1.5 mm glass seed beads.

4. Attach the soft wire to the rope by winding it tightly around the end of the cut length.

   Now begin to carefully wind the beaded wire evenly around the rope, making sure to keep the tension the same throughout.

5. Continue to wind the beaded wire around the rope until you have about 2.4 in. (6 cm) of green beads along the rope.

6. Now, thread a row of brass beads onto your wire. Wind it around the rope in the same way, until you have a 2.8 in. (7 cm) length of brass beads.

3

6

4

5

7. After the row of brass beads, return to the lime-green beads until you have a 2.4 in. (6 cm) length of green beads wound around the rope.

Finish by winding the wire tightly around the rope to secure it as you did at the start.

8. Place a bead end cup over the beaded rope and pull the wire running through the center of the rope through the hole in the cup.

9. Create a loop, using your roundnose pliers (see pages 19–20). (9a, 9b)

10. Repeat the same finishing process at the other end of the rope.

Savannah Zebra Earrings ●●

Created by Noolkitoip

TOOLS & MATERIALS

Wire cutters

Black and white seed beads, 11/0 (1.8 mm)
Handmade 2 mm Ethiopian brass beads
Lime-green seed beads, 11/0 (1.8 mm)
24-gauge hard wire
24-gauge soft wire

1. Using about a 5.9 in. (15 cm) length of 24-gauge hard brass wire, carefully bend it in the middle into a V shape.

2. Next, take a length of 24-gauge soft wire and attach it to one side of the V-shaped hard wire, by winding it tightly around.

3. Thread a 2 mm brass bead onto the soft wire attached to the V shape, and pull it to the central point of the V.

4. Now, wind the soft beaded wire around the other side of the V shape to attach it. This can be a bit fiddly!

   Break off any excess wire.

5. Create a second row of beads by threading two brass beads onto the soft wire. Attach it close to the first row, using the same method as above. (5a, 5b, 5c)

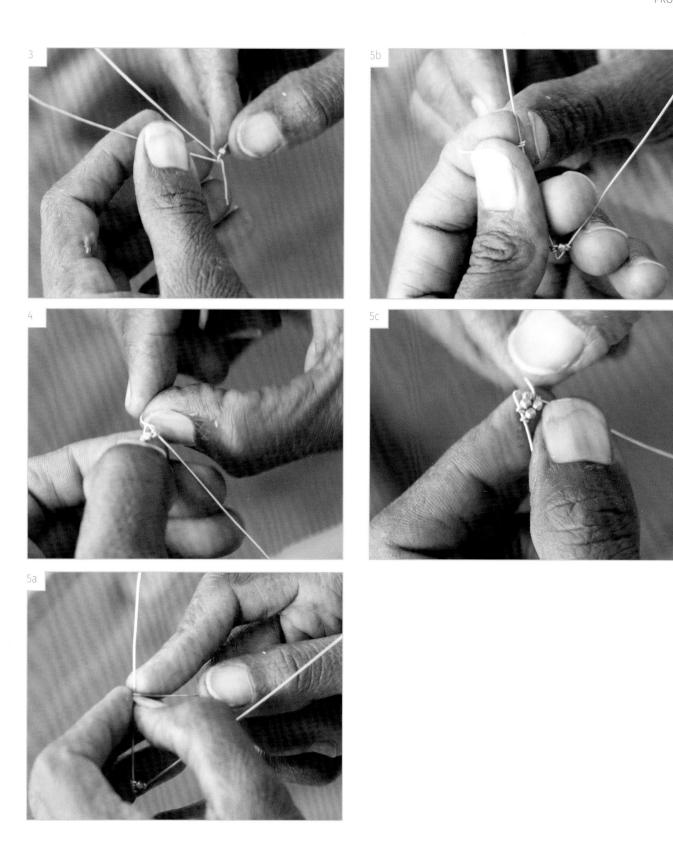

6. Now create a third row of brass beads, using exactly the same method to attach it to the V shape. (6a, 6b)

7. Still using the same method, thread a row of 1.5 mm lime-green glass seed beads and attach it to the V shape next to the brass beads. (7a, 7b)

8. Continue to make five rows of lime-green seed beads, and one row of brass beads, using exactly the same technique as previously.

9. Finally, thread a row of black and white beads and attach them just above the last brass row. Break off any excess wire. (9a, 9b)

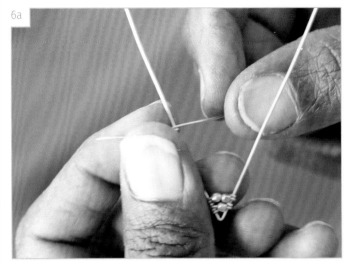
6a

6b

10. Finally, carefully bend the excess wire at the top of your V shape toward the point of the V-shaped wire. Be careful not to break the wire, since this holds all the rows of beads in place.

11. Using your wire cutters, carefully cut the hard wire close to the top row of beads, making sure you have left enough wire to secure the beads in place.

12. Once you have completed your earring, repeat the process to make the second of your pair. Attach the earring hooks. (See step 12, page 34)

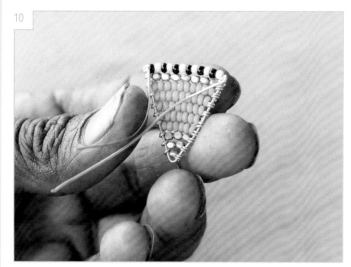

Savannah Semicircle Necklace ●●●

Created by Noolepeta

TOOLS & MATERIALS

Roundnose pliers

Gold stardust bead, 6 mm
Handmade 2 mm Ethiopian brass beads
Lime-green glass seed beads, 11/0 (1.8 mm)
Lobster clasp
22-gauge hard wire
24-gauge soft wire
26-gauge very soft wire

1. Take a length of 22-gauge hard brass wire and thread a 6 mm gold-plated stardust bead into the middle of the wire.

2. Attach a length of soft 24-gauge brass wire by winding it tightly once or twice around the original hard wire. Gently wiggle the wire and break off any excess.

3. Once attached, thread four handmade 2 mm brass beads onto the soft wire.

4. Bend the beaded wire halfway around the stardust bead and attach it securely to the hard wire (using the same method as you used in step 2).

5. Next, thread two more beads onto the soft wire and begin to bend it to surround the central larger bead. Now attach a length of very soft 26-gauge wire, using the same method.

6. Thread two more beads onto the wire and finish surrounding the larger central bead.

7. Wind the beaded wire around the hard wire to attach it securely.

8. Break off any excess wire. You should be left with a stardust bead surrounded by tiny brass beads. Also, a length of very soft 22-gauge brass wire should be attached at right angles to the hard wire running through the central bead.

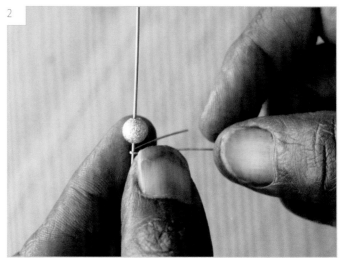

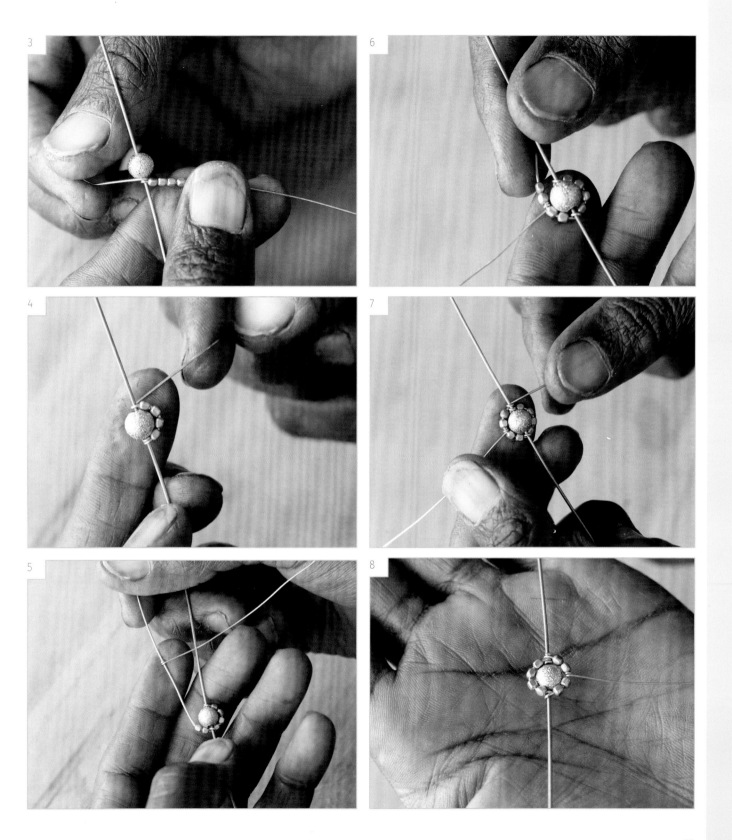

9. Take another length of soft 24-gauge wire and attach it to the central hard wire in the same way as before.

10. Now thread a row of 1.5 mm lime-green beads onto the wire and bend it carefully around the row of brass beads.

   Before you attach it to create a semicircle, take the soft wire (which is secured to the brass-beaded wire) and wind it once around the green-beaded wire in the middle of the row of beads. Leave a length of wire ready to use to secure the next row of beads in place.

11. Complete the first row of green beads by attaching the beaded wire to the central hard wire.

12. Begin the process again, by attaching a length of soft 24-gauge wire to the hard wire running through the large central bead.

13. Again, thread a row of lime-green beads onto the wire and secure it in the center by winding the soft wire (at right angles to the central hard wire) once around the green-beaded wire. Continue until you have another semicircle of lime-green beads next to the previous row.

14. Repeat, by attaching a 24-gauge length of soft wire to the hard wire running through the large central bead. Thread with lime-green beads.

15. Continue the process until you have three rows of lime-green beads in a semicircle around the central bead.

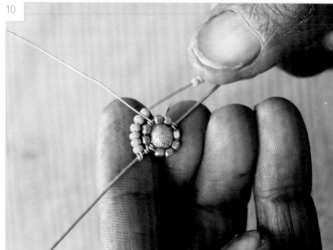

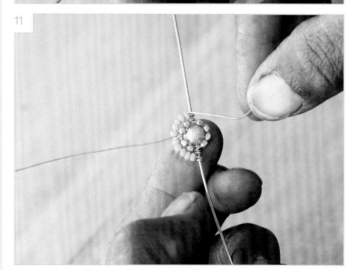

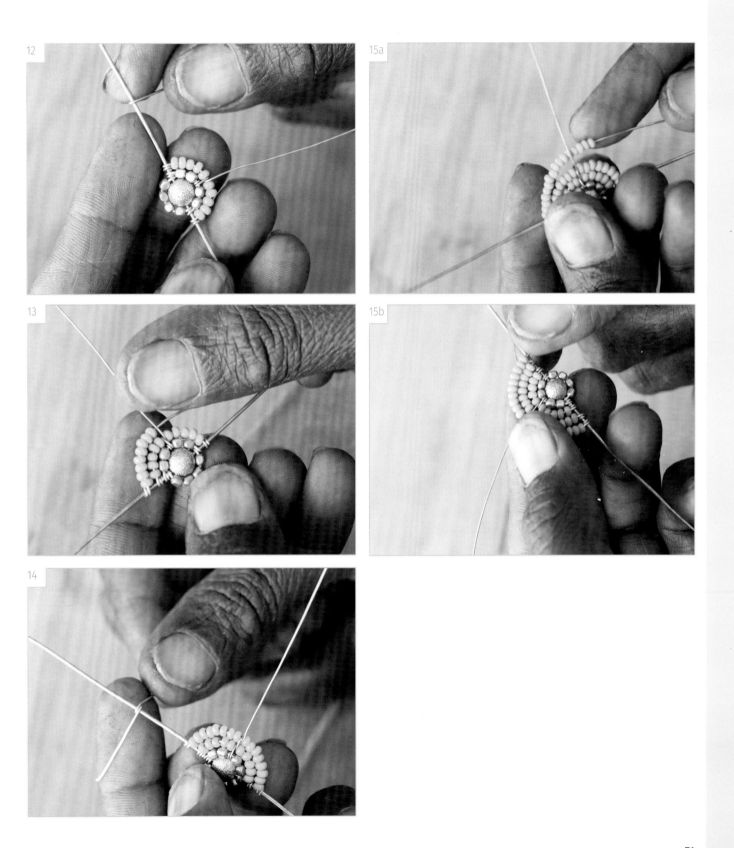

16. Continue with the same method. After you have attached three rows of lime-green beads, attach another two rows of 2 mm brass beads, Break off any excess wire—including the soft wire running through the center of the semicircle. (16a, 16b)

17. Taking your roundnose pliers, make a loop (see page 19), using the hard wire running through the large central bead on each side of the semicircle.

18. Your pendant is now ready for your chain. (see pages 26-27). continue this process until your chain reaches the desired length.

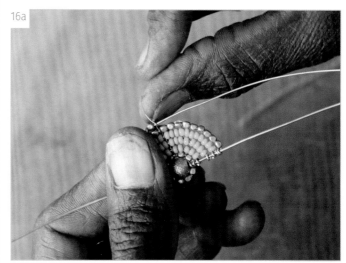

16a

16b

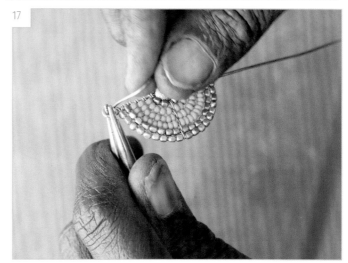

17

Naivasha Teardrop Earrings ●

Created by Noolari

TOOLS & MATERIALS

Flat-nose pliers
Roundnose pliers

Handmade 2 mm Ethiopian brass beads
Turquoise seed beads, 11/0 (1.8 mm)
24-gauge hard wire

1. Cut a length of approximately 7.9 in. (20 cm) of 24-gauge hard brass wire. Thread a row of around 3 cm turquoise beads. Bend the end of the wire to stop the beads from falling off.

2. Next thread a 1.6 in. (4 cm) row of brass beads.

3. Thread another 2 in. (3 cm) row of turquoise beads following the brass beads.

4. Bend the wire into a teardrop shape and secure it together by winding one end of the wire once around the other end, tightly and close to the beads.

5. Break off the excess wire, leaving a length of wire for the next step.

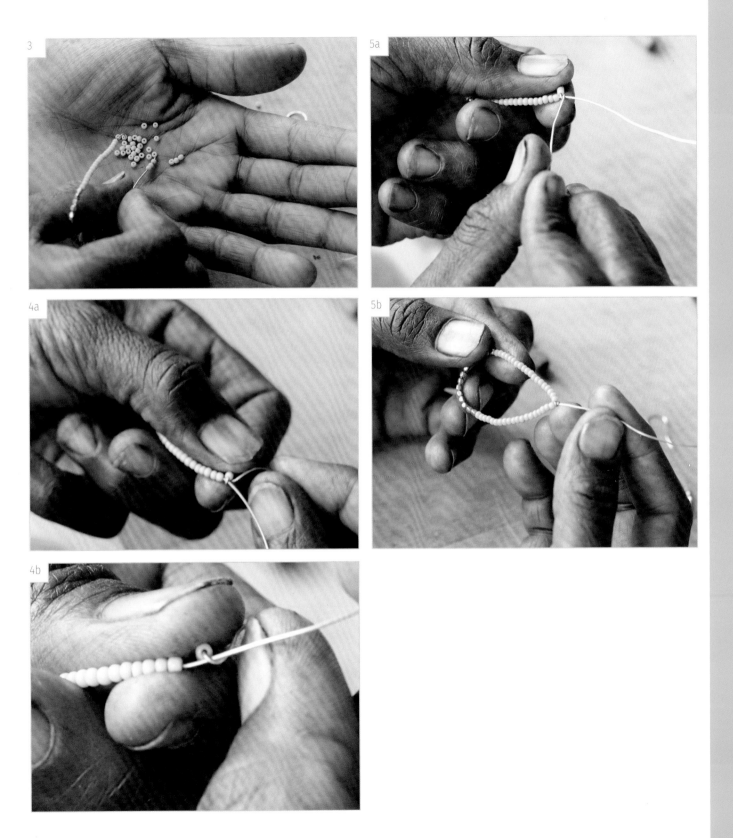

6. Create a loop, using the length of wire left at the top of your teardrop shape. (6a, 6b)

7. You can shape your earring by gently bending the wire so that it is even and symmetrical.

8. Repeat the process to create a pair. Gently bend the wire of the second earring to match the form of the first one. Finally, attach your earring hooks, using your flat-nose pliers. (See step 12, page 34)

6a

6b

7

8

Naivasha Pearl Necklace ●●

Created by Noolari

TOOLS & MATERIALS

Beading awl
Roundnose pliers

Brass head pin or 24-gauge hard wire
Brass lobster clasp
Freshwater pearl, grade A, 6–8 mm
Handmade 2 mm Ethiopian brass beads
Turquoise seed beads, 11/0 (1.8 mm)
24-gauge soft wire

1. Thread a 6–8 mm freshwater pearl onto a brass head pin (or you can use hard wire with a bent and pinched end to create a bead stop).

2. Next, wind a piece of 24-gauge soft wire tightly around your head pin to attach and secure it.

3. Thread a small row of turquoise beads onto your soft wire.

4. Now surround your pearl with turquoise beads (see pages 22-23).

5. Once you have secured the turquoise-beaded wire onto your head pin, thread a small row of 2 mm brass beads onto the wire. Carefully bend it around the turquoise bead surround. (5a, 5b)

   Secure it by winding the soft wire tightly around the head pin, breaking off any excess wire.

6. Next, using your roundnose pliers, create a loop onto the pin head. Make sure your loop is big enough to allow you to feed your chain through so it can hang freely. (6a, 6b)

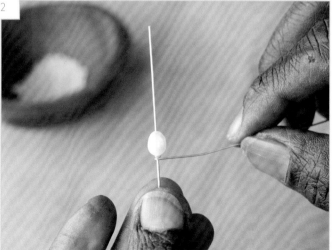

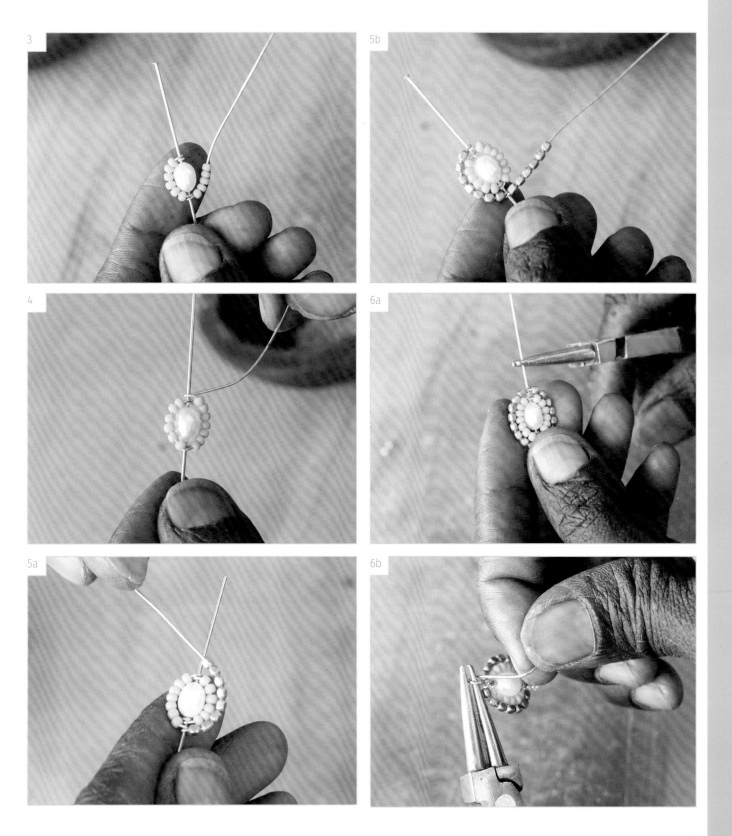

7. Your pendant is now ready for your chain. (see pages 26-27). continue this process until your chain reaches the desired length. Finally, thread your beaded chain.

8. Attach your lobster clasp (see page 21) and your extension chain (see pages 28-29).

Naivasha Pearl Bracelet ●●

Created by Noolari

TOOLS & MATERIALS

Beading awl
Roundnose pliers

Brass lobster clasp
Freshwater pearl, grade A, 8–9 mm
Gold stardust bead, 8 mm
Gold stardust beads, 2 x 4 mm
Handmade 2 mm Ethiopian brass beads
Turquoise stone beads, 1 x 4 mm, 1 x 6 mm,
    1 x 8 mm
24-gauge hard wire
24-gauge soft wire

1. Thread a row of 2 mm brass beads onto a length of 24-gauge hard wire. Make beaded linked rings by referring to the technique on pages 24–25.

2. Taking another length of hard 24-gauge wire: thread one 4 mm turquoise stone bead, followed by one 6 mm turquoise stone bead, one 8 mm turquoise stone bead, and one 4 mm gold stardust bead.

3. Create a chain link from the smaller beaded ring to your hard wire (see pages 24–25).

   Now, using the technique to create a beaded surround (see pages 22-23), attach your soft wire, then surround the 8 mm turquoise bead with 2 mm brass beads.

4. On the same wire, create another bead surround, this time using a 6 mm turquoise central bead and surrounding it with brass beads.

5. Continue this process, using the same technique, and surround a 4 mm turquoise bead with brass beads. Following this, surround a 4 mm gold stardust bead, also with brass beads.

6. Next, link your bead surrounds together, using the beaded chain technique (see pages 26–27). (6a, 6b, 6c, and 6d overleaf)

7. Next, attach another length of hard 24-gauge wire.

8. Thread and surround your pearl with 2 mm brass beads. Do the same with a 6 mm gold stardust bead, and last, surround a 4 mm gold stardust bead with brass beads.

9. Create a chain link between each of your bead surrounds.

10. Finally attach your lobster clasp and extension chain to finish.

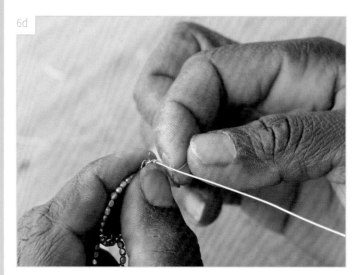

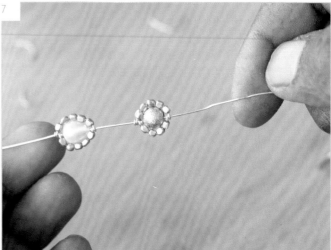

Zebra Necklace in Blue, Turquoise, and Magenta ●

Created by Noolari

TOOLS & MATERIALS

Beading awl
Flat-nose pliers
Roundnose pliers

Crimp beads
Gold-plated stardust beads, 3 x 4 mm
Handmade 2 mm Ethiopian brass beads
Magenta glass bead, 4 mm
Nylon-coated beading wire
Raw brass lobster clasp
Seed beads in turquoise, black, white, and
    royal blue, 11/0 (1.8 mm)
24-gauge soft wire

1. Cut about 15.5 in. (40 cm) of nylon-coated beading wire. This type of wire is composed of strands of thin brass wire twisted together and coated with nylon. It is strong and flexible and hangs nicely.

    Thread a crimp bead onto the end. These are soft metal beads used to secure loops.

2. Create a small loop with your beading wire by carefully passing the end of the wire back through the brass crimp, using flat-nosed pliers. Line up the crimp in the tip of your pliers as straight as possible; hold the pliers at a right angle to the wire, then carefully squeeze down on the pliers and squash the crimp flat. Your loop should now be secure and permanent.

3. You are ready to start threading your beads onto the wire. The crimp bead will stop the beads from falling off. (3a, 3b)

    Your first few beads will cover the loose end of the wire after the crimp bead.

Begin by threading:
    1.5 in. (4 cm) length of royal-blue beads
    3 x 2 mm brass beads
    3.9 in. (10 cm) length of black and white seed beads
    1 x 4 mm magenta bead
    3 x 2 mm brass beads
    2.4 in. (6 cm) length of 1.5 mm turquoise beads
    3 x 4 mm gold-plated stardust beads
    1 in. (2.5 cm) length of royal-blue beads
    3.9 in. (10 cm) length of 2 mm brass beads
    1.5 in. (4 cm) length of 1.5 mm turquoise beads

4. Once you have threaded all your beads, you can create another loop at the other end of the wire to secure the beads—and later to attach your clasp (see page 21). (4a, 4b)

Now you are ready to attach your clasp and extension chain.

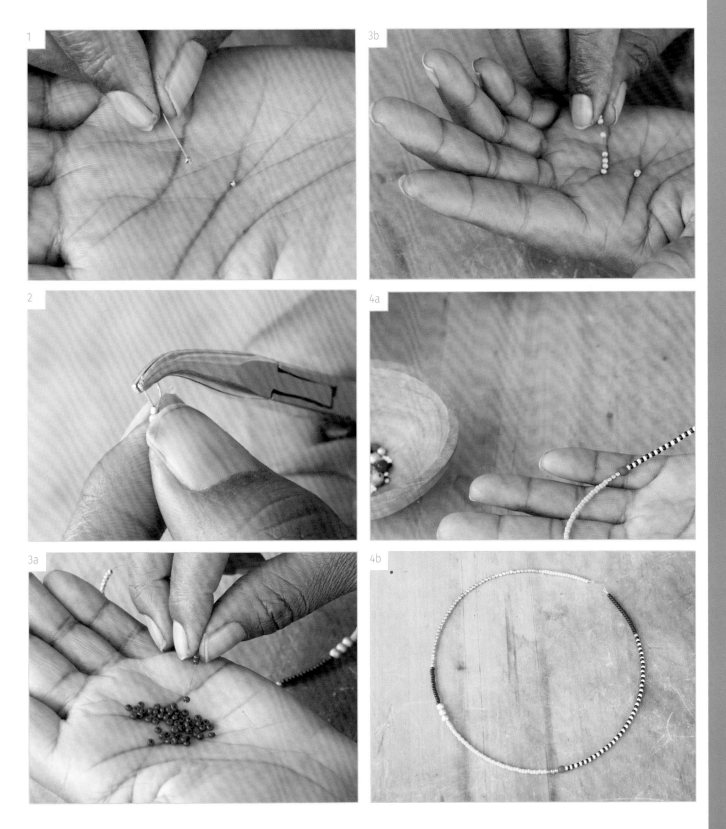

5. Take a length of about 5.9 in. (15 cm) 24-gauge soft brass wire and begin an extension chain on one of the loops of the beaded necklace (see pages 28–29, "Creating an Extension Chain"). You can make your extension chain as long or as short as you like.

6. Finally, attach a brass bead and the lobster clasp on the other end of your necklace to finish.

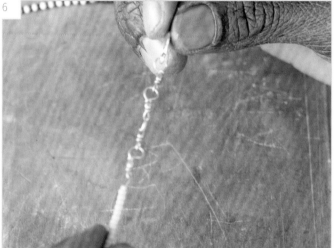

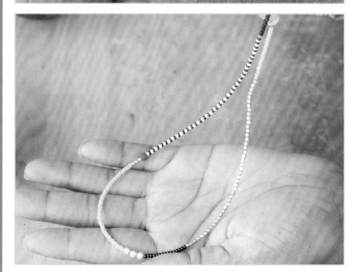

Zebra Bracelet in Blue, Turquoise, and Magenta ●●

Created by Noomishuki

TOOLS & MATERIALS

Beading awl

Roundnose pliers

Black and white seed beads, 11/0 (1.8 mm)

Blue seed beads, 11/0 (1.8 mm)

Gold stardust beads, 2 x 4 mm

Handmade 2 mm Ethiopian brass beads

Lobster clasp

Magenta glass beads, 2 x 4 mm

Royal-blue glass beads, 2 x 4 mm

Turquoise beads, 2 x 4 mm

24-gauge soft wire

1. For this beaded bracelet, you need to refer to pages 22–23, "Creating a Beaded Surround," for the method. Follow the color pattern of the beads in the image to create a balance of bright color with gold beads in between.

   Take a length of 24-gauge hard wire and thread one of your 4 mm beads onto it. Create a beaded surround (see pages 22–23).

2. Now create a seed bead circle on your central wire (see pages 20–21).

3. Use the central wire to create beaded surrounds with each of the 4 mm beads in the design, plus two gold seed bead circles. (3a)

In this design, we used the following pattern:

A) Blue bead with gold-beaded surround

B) Gold stardust bead with gold-beaded surround

C) Turquoise bead with gold-beaded surround

D) Gold seed bead circle

E) Magenta bead with black-and-white-beaded surround

F) Gold stardust bead with gold-beaded surround

G) Blue bead with gold-beaded surround

H) Gold seed bead circle

I) Magenta bead with black-and-white-beaded surround

J) Gold stardust bead with gold-beaded surround

K) Turquoise bead with gold-beaded surround

4. Now you can link each of your bead surrounds and seed bead circles and create a chain (see pages 26–27). (4a, 4b)

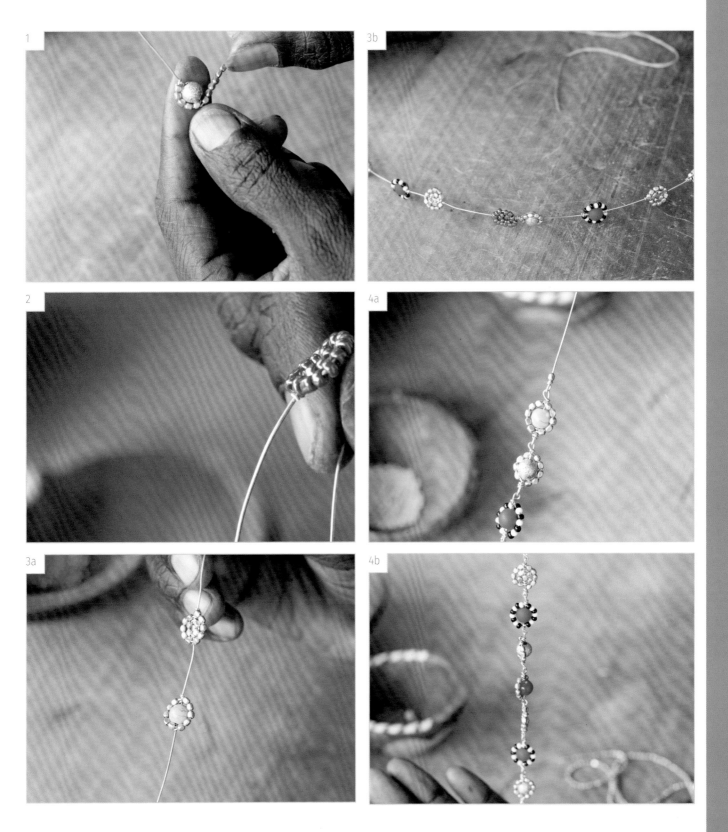

5. Attach a 2 mm brass seed bead and chain link, then attach the lobster clasp. The Maasai artisans often use their beading awl to create a tiny loop, but you may find it easier to use your roundnose pliers.

6. At the opposite end, again add a 2 mm brass bead and create an extension, using your roundnose pliers. (6a, 6b)

Zebra Earrings in Blue, Turquoise, and Magenta ●●●

Created by Melau

TOOLS & MATERIALS

Beading awl
Craft knife
Roundnose pliers
Wire cutters

Black and white beads, 11/0 (1.8 mm)
Black plastic recycled water container
Blue glass seed beads, 11/0 (1.8 mm)
Brass pin, 2 in. (5.5 cm)
Handmade 2 mm Ethiopian brass beads
Magenta glass beads, 4 mm
Turquoise glass seed beads, 11/0 (1.8 mm)
24-gauge soft wire

1. Using a craft knife, cut four 0.2 in. wide by 1.2 in. long (0.5 mm x 3 cm) pieces of black (robust but bendy) plastic. (1a, 1b, 1c)

2. Thread a 4 mm magenta bead onto a brass or gold-plated head pin. (2a)

   Attach a length of 24-gauge brass wire to the pin just under the bead (see pages 22-23). (2b)

3. Using your beading awl, make a hole about 2 mm from one end of your first piece of plastic. (3a, 3b)

4. Taking the wire you have attached to the pin (under the pink bead), thread a couple of blue seed beads onto it.

1a

1b

5. Now feed the same piece of wire through the plastic hole you have made, and pull the plastic along the wire toward the two blue beads. (5a, 5b)

6. Now take the same wire and thread two more blue beads onto it. Attach it to the pin by winding it tightly around it once.

7. Continue the process by threading two more beads onto the same wire.

   Feed it through the second piece of plastic. Pull the plastic along the wire until it's right next to the beads. Now add two more blue beads.

   Wind the wire tightly around the pin once to attach it, but leave a length of wire to thread your next row of beads.

8. Next, pierce a hole about 1–1.5 mm away from the row of blue beads. Thread four or five turquoise beads onto your wire.

9. Feed the beaded wire through the hole you have made in the plastic. Pull it tight, so that the row of turquoise beads is nestled next to the blue beads.

10. Repeat this process until you have surrounded the first row of blue beads with a row of turquoise beads.

11. Wind the wire once around the pin to attach it, making sure you leave a length of wire ready for your next row of beads.

12. Thread a row of black and white 1.5 mm seed beads onto your wire.

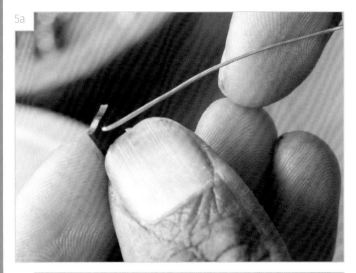

5a

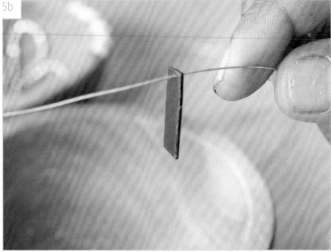

5b

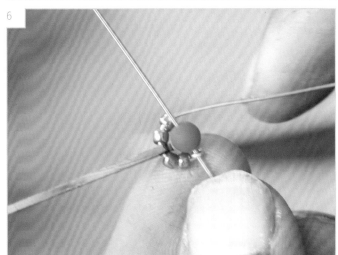

6

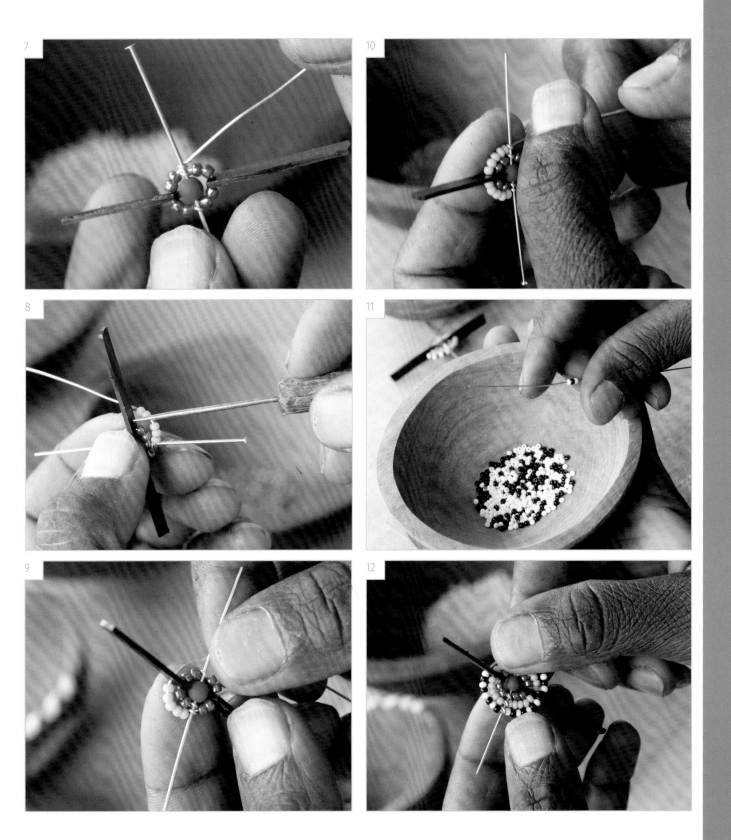

13. Using the same technique as before, make holes in both pieces of plastic and feed your black-and-white-beaded wire through. Then pull it tight toward the row of turquoise beads.

14. Wind the wire once around the pin (as before) to attach it, leaving a length of wire ready for threading your final row of beads.

    NB. Wind the wire in the same direction as before so that you create a tidy and even circle.

15. Thread a row of brass beads onto your wire.

16. Again, pierce holes in both sides of the plastic strip, close to the row of black and white beads.

17. Feed your beaded wire through the first plastic strip, again pulling it close to the previous row of beads.

18. Finish your final row of brass beads and attach it to the pin in the same way as before, but this time wind it another halfway around. Break off any excess wire.

19. Using your roundnose pliers to grip the head pin, pull the beaded circle to the bottom.

20. Create a loop at the top of the beaded circle.

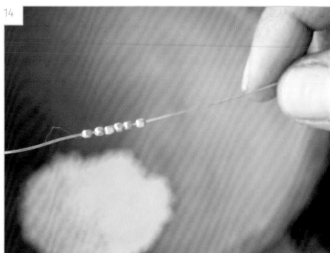

21. Cut off any excess wire—you will need to use a wire cutter, since the head pin can be quite stiff to bend using just your fingers.

   With your craft knife, trim away any excess plastic. (21a, 21b)

22. Attach your earring hook and repeat the process to complete the pair! (see step 12, page 34)

21a

21b

22

Flamingo Earrings ●

Created by Sikar

TOOLS & MATERIALS

Flat-nose pliers
Roundnose pliers
Wire cutters

Dark-coral glass seed beads, 11/0 (1.8 mm)
Handmade 2 mm Ethiopian brass beads
Ivory glass seed beads, 11/0 (1.8 mm)
Light-coral glass seed beads, 11/0 (1.8 mm)
24-gauge hard wire

1. Cut three lengths of about 2.4–3 in. (6–8 cm) hard brass wire.

    Now, using your bent/flat-nose pliers, bend the tips of each piece of wire and pinch to create bead stops. (1a, 1b)

2. Thread a mix of light-coral, dark-coral, ivory, and brass seed beads onto each of your three wires.

    One wire should have about 1 in. (2.5 cm) of mixed beads, and the two other wires should have about 0.8 in. (2 cm) matching rows of beads.

3. Now, taking your roundnose pliers, create a loop on the open end of each of the beaded pins (see pages 19–20). (3a, 3b, 3c)

4. Next, take a roughly 4.7 in. (12 cm) length of 24-gauge hard wire and thread it with 2 mm brass beads. Carefully bend it into a 1 in. (2.5 cm) diameter ring. Cross over and wind the wire around itself to secure it, leaving a short length of wire to create a loop later.

5. Once you have created a ring, pull the length of wire out of the tiny attachment loop you have just created.

1a

1b

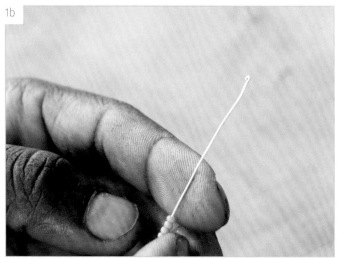

6. Feed your beaded open ring through the loops on your mixed beaded pins. Start with one of the short pins first, then the longer pin, and last the other short-beaded pin. Now, feed the length of wire back through your tiny attachment loop. (6a, 6b)

7. Now, create a loop with the wire left at the top of your beaded ring.

8. Repeat the process—following the color order of the beads—to create another earring to make up the pair.

9. Finally, attach your earring hooks, using your flat-nose pliers. (See step 12, page 34)

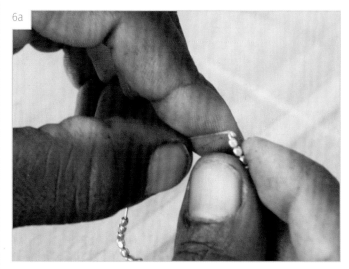

6a

6b

7

8
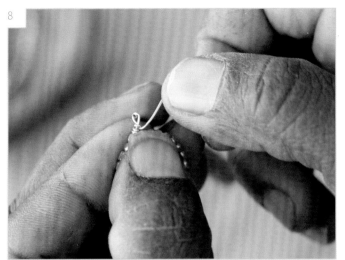

9

Flamingo Necklace ●●

Created by Sikar

TOOLS & MATERIALS

Bent roundnose pliers
Roundnose pliers

Brass cowrie shell
Freshwater pearl, 6–8 mm
Handmade 2 mm Ethiopian brass beads
Ivory, light-coral, dark-coral glass seed beads,
   11/0 (1.8 mm)
Lobster clasp
24-gauge hard wire
24-gauge soft wire

For this necklace, you can refer to the step-by-step guide to making the Flamingo Earrings. They work brilliantly as a set, and creating them involves a similar construction method.

1. Begin by creating a brass-beaded ring (see pages 24–25) and make just one ring of 1–1.2 in. (2.5–3 cm) diameter. This is exactly the same as one of the beaded rings used for the Flamingo Earrings. Create a loop at the top of the ring.

2. Next, take a brass cowrie shell and feed about a 4.7 in. (12 cm) length of soft 24-gauge wire through the wide end of the slit, and down through the center of the shell. Now, in the same way as you have done before, secure it by looping the wire around the shell and then winding the wire twice around itself.

   Break off any excess wire, leaving a length long enough to create a loop.

3. Taking the cowrie shell, attach it loosely to your beaded ring by creating a loop (see page 19) around the ring, using roundnose pliers. Attaching it loosely will let it hang freely and allow for some movement. Break off any excess wire.

4. Now cut three lengths of around 2.4–3 in. (6–8 cm) hard brass wire. Now, using your bent/flat-nose pliers, bend the tips of each piece of wire and pinch it to create bead stops.

5. Thread a mix of ivory, light-coral, dark-coral, and brass seed beads onto two of your wires. One wire should have a 1 in. (2.5 cm) row of mixed beads, and the other wire should have about 0.8 in. (2 cm) row of beads. See the Flamingo Earring project; you can use exactly the same method. (5a, 5b)

6. Attach the beaded pins to your ring one by one. This creates a loop around the ring. Secure it, using the same technique as you did to attach the cowrie shell.

7. Next, thread a 6–8 mm freshwater pearl onto one of the wires (secured with a bead end stop).

8. Attach the pearl to your beaded ring in the same way as you attached the shell and beaded pins. Break off any excess wire.

9. After attaching the cowrie shell, the two beaded pins, and the pearl, you can thread a beaded chain through the loop created on the brass-beaded ring. See pages 26–27, "Creating a Beaded Chain," to show you how to make one. Now attach a lobster clasp. Finally, create an extension chain to attach your clasp to. (9a, 9b, 9c)

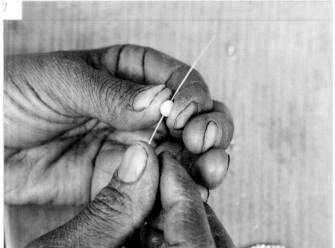

9a

9c

9b

White Arrowhead Earrings ●●

Created by Noolturot

TOOLS & MATERIALS

Beading awl
Roundnose pliers

Handmade 2 mm Ethiopian brass beads
White seed beads, 11/0 (1.8mm)
24-gauge hard wire
24-gauge soft wire
26-gauge soft wire

1. Thread a length of 1.2–1.4 in. (3–3.5 cm) of 24-gauge hard wire with brass beads. This will be about fourteen beads.

2. Create a V shape with the beaded wire.

3. Cut a length of about 5.9 in. (15 cm) of 24-gauge soft wire. Thread onto it about 1 in. (2 cm) of white 1.5 mm beads (approximately twelve beads).

4. Now attach your white-beaded wire to both sides of your V shape and bend it into an upside-down, wide V shape. Attach a length of 26-gauge soft wire to the center of the row of white beads. This will secure the rows of beads you are about to add.

5. Continue the process by adding two more rows of white beads above the first row. Now create a small loop in the soft 26-gauge wire you have used to secure the three rows of beads.

   NB. Your loop can be small, because you won't need to thread a chain through the eye.

6. Now bend the excess wire on both sides of the larger V shape and cut them off, using wire cutters.

   Repeat the process, creating another beaded arrowhead earring.

   Finally, attach the earring hooks to the little loops at the top. (See step 12, page 34)

3a

4b

4

5

White Arrowhead Necklace ●●

Created by Noolari

TOOLS & MATERIALS

Beading awl
Roundnose pliers

Handmade 2 mm Ethiopian brass beads
White glass seed beads, 11/0 (1.8 mm)
24-gauge hard wire
24-gauge soft wire
26–28-gauge soft wire

1. Using a length of 24-gauge hard wire, thread approximately 2.4–2.8 in. (6–7 cm) length of handmade brass beads.

   Carefully bend the beaded wire in the middle of the row.

2. Create a V shape.

3. Using soft wire, thread approximately 1 in. (2.5 cm) of 2 mm white glass seed beads.

4. Attach the soft white-beaded wire to one side of the brass-beaded hard wire by winding it tightly around at the top of the row of brass beads.

5. Now, stretch the white-beaded wire across to the other side of the V-shaped brass-beaded wire.

6. Bend the white-beaded wire into a wide, upside-down V shape and attach it to the hard wire just above the brass beads.

7. In the same way, attach a second row of white beads just above the first row, bending it to follow the first row.

8. Continue the process by adding a third row of white beads. You will begin to see your pendant taking shape.

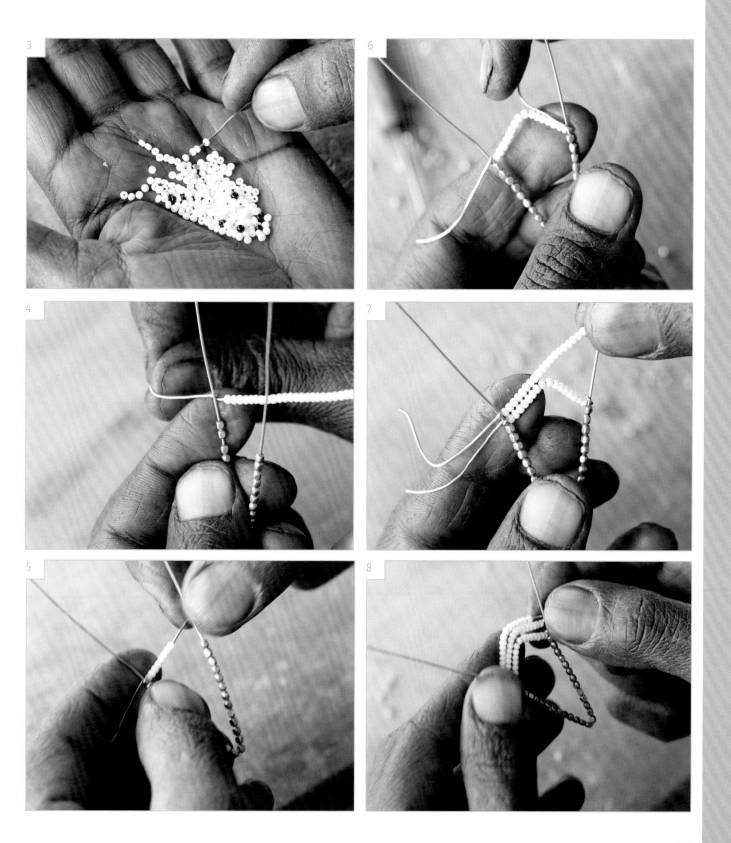

9. To secure the three rows of beads, take some very thin (26–28 gauge) soft wire and thread it through the middle of the bottom row of white beads at the point of the V shape. Attach it tightly by winding it twice around the beaded wire.

10. Continue the process by winding the very thin wire around the wire holding the next row of white beads above the first.

    Pull it tightly to secure the rows of beads.

11. Continue the process by tightly winding the thin wire through the center of the top row of white beads.

    It should be securely held in place now, so the shape will remain intact.

12. Using the remaining thin wire, create a loop at the top. This needs to be big enough to thread your beaded chain through and for it to move around and hang freely.

    Bend the excess wire on both sides of the large V-shaped beaded pendant.

13. Using your wire cutters, carefully cut the wire on both sides, making sure you have left enough wire to hold the white-beaded wires in place.

14. Finally, feed your handmade beaded chain through the loop at the top of your pendant and finish with an extension chain and lobster clasp.

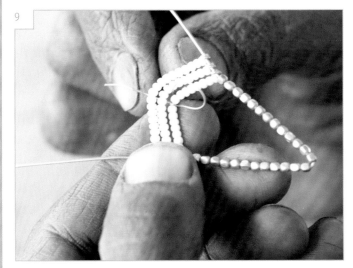

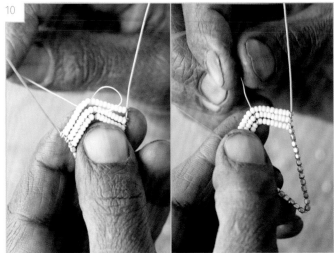

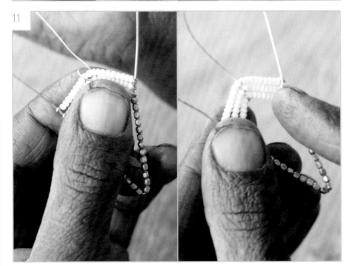

12

13a

13b

14

White-and-Gold Geometric Cuff Bracelet ●●●

Created by Noolepeta

TOOLS & MATERIALS

Beading awl
Craft knife
Wire cutters

Handmade 2 mm Ethiopian brass beads
White recycled plastic bottle
White seed beads, 11/0 (1.8 mm)
24-gauge hard wire

1. Take a white plastic bottle or something similar you can recycle and use; however, it needs to be fairly bendy and robust. The Maasai use old plastic bottles of the kind they use to collect water from the river.

2. Using a craft knife, cut a square about 0.8 x 0.8 in. (2 x 2 cm).

3. You can also prepare strips of plastic approximately 0.2 in. (0.5 cm) wide.

   Using your beading awl, pierce holes at an angle starting a few millimeters from one end of the square.

4. The holes need to go all the way through the plastic.

5. Now bend two 9.5 in. (24 cm) lengths of 24-gauge hard wire in half.

6. Feed both ends of one of your pieces of wire into two of the holes you have made in the plastic square.

7. Repeat the process with your second piece of wire. Pull them both through until the folds in the wires are tight against the plastic and form a loop.

8. Take a third length of wire and push it through the last hold in the plastic.

9. Now, bend and feed it through the loop next to it on the plastic. Pull tightly to secure it. Break off any excess wire.

10. You should have five lengths of wire ready for threading your seed beads onto.

11. Begin threading 1.5 mm white glass seed beads onto each wire.

12. Thread about nine beads onto each wire. Then take your strip of plastic in one hand and the beading awl in the other and make five tiny holes (approximately 3 mm apart) in a row down the center of the strip.

13. Feed each piece of wire through the holes in your plastic strip and pull it tight—up tight to your threaded beads, so it secures the beads in place and acts as a divider.

14. Continue threading your wires with beads. In this section, you are creating a gold triangle, using 2 mm brass beads.

15. First, feed your white seed beads onto the wires, starting with one bead on the first wire, two on the second wire, and so on until the last wire has five beads. This is the beginning of your first triangle.

16. Next, thread 2 mm brass beads onto the wires to create a triangle.

Please note that because the beads are handmade, they can vary in size, so you may find that you need to add or take away a bead to make it fit. This will not affect the overall feel and design of the finished cuff.

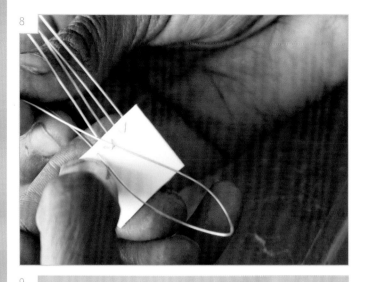

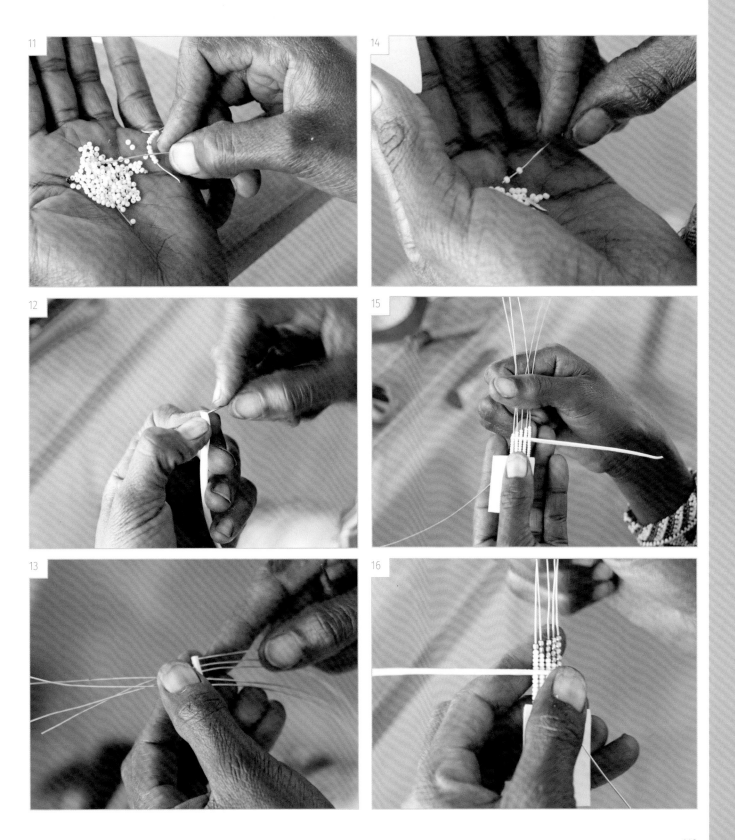

17. Continue the process until you have created a gold triangle contrasted by white beads.

18. Add your next plastic divider, using the same method as previously.

19. For your next section, use white beads. (18a, 18b)

20. Cut off any excess plastic and use it for your next divider.

21. Continue this process creating gold triangles, alternately changing their direction and surrounding them with white beads. Leave a section of white beads between each triangle.

22. Once you have created about twelve sections of beads, you can begin the process of finishing your cuff.

Take your beading awl and make five new holes in your square of plastic. These should line up with your wires.

Begin a few millimeters from the end and pierce the plastic at an angle—coming out at the very edge of the plastic, so the wires will be hidden from the outside of the cuff.

23. Now feed your wires through the holes on the edge of the plastic.

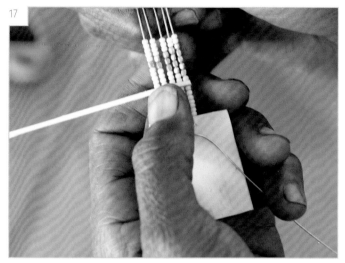

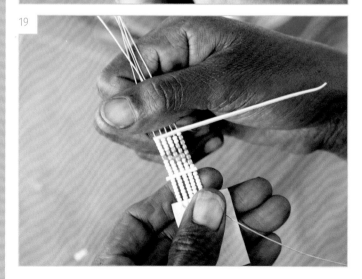

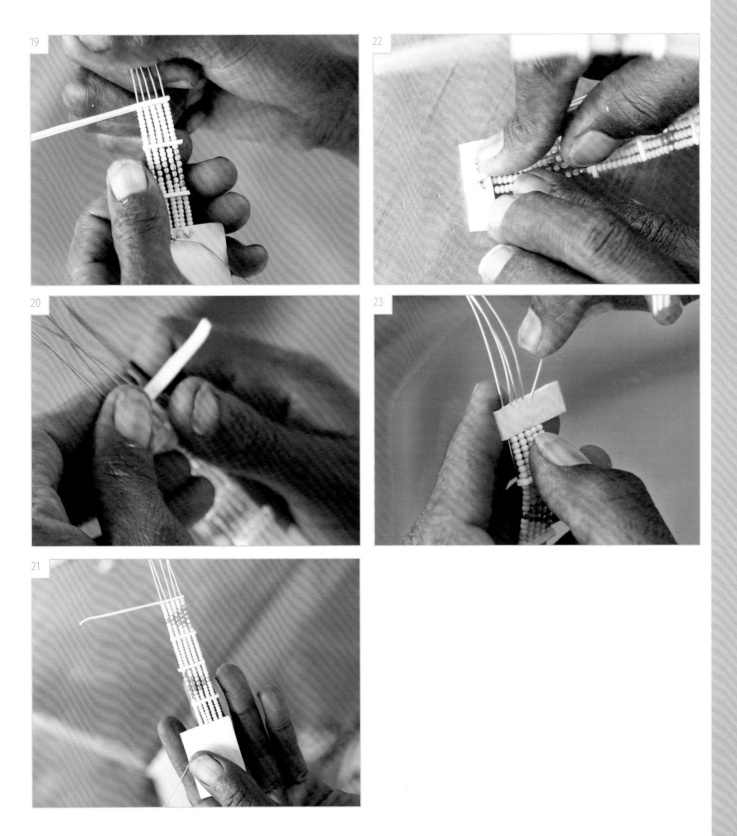

24. Pull your wires from the inside until you join up both ends of your cuff. (24a, 24b)

25. Bend and feed each wire back between the rows of beads and pull until tight.

26. Once the wires have been pulled through to the outside of the cuff, break off the excess wire by twisting and wiggling them back and forth. (26a, 26b)

27. Carefully trim the plastic until it is neat and tidy.

28. Your finished cuff should be easy to slip on and off and hang loosely on your wrist.

24a

24b

25

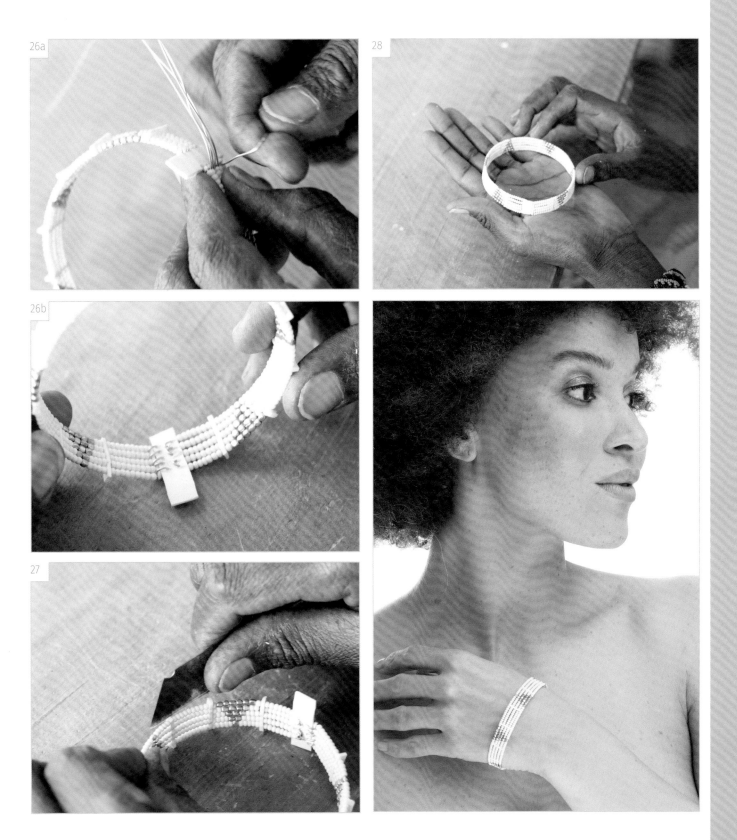

26a

26b

27

28

Arrowhead Ring Earrings ●●

Created by Noolari

TOOLS & MATERIALS

Roundnose pliers

Handmade 2 mm Ethiopian brass beads
White seed beads, 11/0 (1.8 mm)
24-gauge hard wire

1. Thread a roughly 3.9 in. (10 cm) row of white 1 mm seed beads onto a length of around 9.8 in. (25 cm) 24-gauge hard wire. Carefully bend into a circle.

2. Where the beads meet, cross one end of the wire over the other.

3. Take one end of the wire and wrap it tightly around the other to secure it together in a circle. (3a, 3b)

4. Break off any excess wire, leaving a ring of beads and a length of wire you can work with to create a loop. (4a, 4b)

5. Create a loop at the top of the circle, using the roundnose pliers. (5a, 5b)

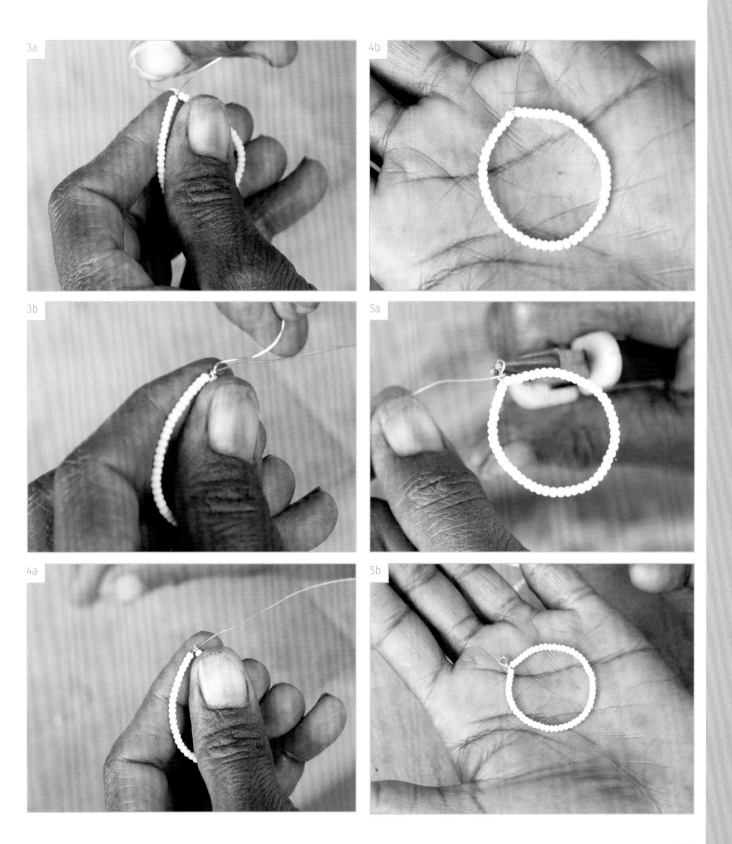

6. Next, create a triangle, using five rows of 2 mm brass beads. You can use exactly the same technique as you used to make your green Zebra Triangle Earrings.

Attach about a 7.9 in. (20 cm) length of 22-gauge soft wire to the triangle by winding it around the center of the top row of beads. Break off any excess wire and leave a length long enough to thread a seed bead and attach it to the white-beaded ring.

7. Thread a white 1 mm seed bead onto the wire attached to the triangle.

8. Next, attach the brass-beaded triangle by winding the wire (you have just attached) around your white-beaded circle, directly parallel to the loop at the top of the circle.

9. Now, wind the wire around itself, just above the white bead next to the beaded circle.

10. Break off any excess wire.

11. Attach an earring hook to the loop at the top of the ring (see step 12, page 34). Repeat the process to create a pair.

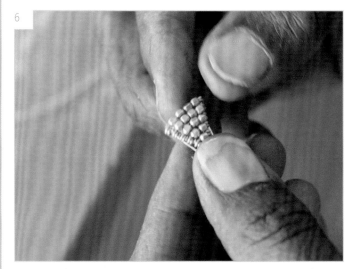

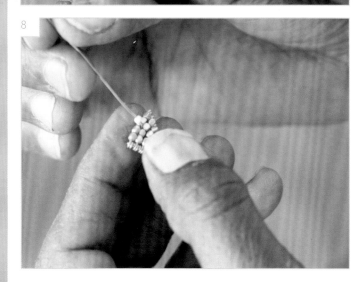

Stockists and suppliers

Etsyshop: Yakutum
Raw brass cowrie shells, raw brass pins, raw brass lobster clasps

www.beadsunlimited.co.uk
Nylon-coated beading wire, crimps, turquoise beads (4, 6, 8 mm), toggle clasp, earring hooks, freshwater pearls

Etsyshop: Julzbeads
Etsyshop: TheLushBeadShop   Stardust beads

Etsyshop: Beads21
Etsyshop: beadsfromCzech
Blue glass beads (6 mm), yellow glass beads (6 mm)

www.the-beadshop.co.uk
Magenta beads (neon orchid), 4, 6, 8 mm

Etsyshop: MetalClays4you
Brass wire

Etsyshop: Thebeadchest
Brass seed beads

www.preciosa.com
Glass seed beads

About the author

From a large and adventurous Anglo-Irish family, Becca has always been fascinated by color and design. After art school and with her love of adventure, she traveled widely and on one journey met her future husband, Hennie, in Jerusalem. After living in South Africa and London, and while their children were still very young, the couple took the bold step of moving to a remote part of southern Kenya to live and work among a traditional Maasai community.

The family quickly assimilated into the local community, where Becca, in particular, bonded with the women. Using her creative skills and love of color, they found common creative ground that turned into a growing international beadwork enterprise called RedTribe. This started from one Maasai widow and a handful of beads.

Their beadwork is based on centuries-old, traditional Maasai materials, colors, and skills. The income generated is used to support and empower the women and help create sustainability for the other projects that Becca and Hennie have developed in partnership with the Maasai. After eleven years living in Kenya, the family moved to south Devon. Becca visits Kenya as often as she can and continues to design new collections with the Maasai artisans of RedTribe. The team there continues to run the Maasai Academy and the clinic, and bringing water to the villages. Find out more by visiting www.redtribe.org.

All proceeds from this book will go toward developing RedTribe beadwork and empowering the artisans.

The Maasai are a seminomadic people, rich in tradition and culture, living across the borders of Kenya and Tanzania. As a result of rapidly changing lifestyle, culture, and climate, the Maasai have become a marginalized community, suffering increasing poverty and having little or no healthcare or education.